A GUIDE TO OLD AMERICAN HOUSES 1700-1900

A GUIDE TO OLD

by Henry Lionel Williams and Ottalie K. Williams

NEW YORK: A. S. Barnes and Company, Inc.

AMERICAN HOUSES

1700-1900

LONDON: Thomas Yoseloff Ltd.

A. S. Barnes and Co., Inc.
South Brunswick, New Jersey

Thomas Yoseloff Ltd.
18 Charing Cross Road
London W. C. 2, England

First Printing, September 1962
Second Printing, April 1963
Third Printing, September 1966
Fourth Printing, July 1967

FRONTISPIECE

A perfect early New England center-chimney house with connecting sheds and barn, an arrangement made necessary by the severe Massachusetts winters: the Abbot Farm, Andover, built around 1660.

9791
Printed in the United States of America

For Mary I. Roberts
who supplied the spark

CONTENTS

A GUIDE TO OLD AMERICAN HOUSES 1700-1900

Introduction

OUR ARCHITECTURAL HERITAGE

Since American colonists started building their first permanent homes in the 17th Century, fashions in houses have changed many times. Most of the surviving old dwellings—even those erected no more than sixty years ago—are likely to have been remodeled or to have had their faces lifted time and again as changing fashions and ideas of convenience demanded. This means that today, unless we have made a study of such things, we may often find it difficult to tell from casual observation just what period or style a house originally belonged to, much less approximate the age of the original structure. The situation can be tantalizing to anyone interested in old houses, professionally or otherwise. On the other hand, the ability to recognize the original architectural style, either of a house or of a public building, and to determine what, if anything, has been done to it since it was first erected, normally is not too difficult once a few basic facts are mastered. And this can be a gratifying as well as a useful accomplishment.

Even in instances where it may not be possible to name the style offhand, the reader will be able to understand what he is looking at because he will know where and how the architectural details originated and what they represent.

In studying the basic styles, however, it must be realized that very few houses exist today that can be presented as "pure" examples of any one architectural design. There may be several variations of each, all equally good from an architectural standpoint, but representing modifications due to differing interior arrangements, building proportions, window placement (fenestration), or merely to decorative treatment. It is such things that give each house its individuality, and enable us to recognize the work of some particular artisan or architect. These variations, which in some instances may go as far as the number and arrangement of chimneys or the kind of roof, may seem to make positive identification of the basic style more difficult, but if we are familiar with the determining features we cannot go far wrong.

On the other hand, we do have to remember that even the type of construction used may be deceptive. Log-walled or half-timbered houses (as distinct from those having a braced frame), which we should expect to find in

11

very early construction, were occasionally built as late as the 19th century.

In order to be able to decide whether some specific house is an authentic period piece or merely an original mongrel, it is first necessary to know something about the more obvious characteristics of the various basic architectural styles, and the commoner variations that became popular between the years 1700 and 1900. This period is chosen as being the one during which structural features were more or less settled and a natural progression of definite architectural styles established.

By tracing the evolution of these styles and noting the introduction of new ones during that time we can learn to detect what was added and what was altered, and so recognize the basic structure. However, we also have to remember that placing the style and period is but the first step in determining just what it is that we are looking at. Many old houses were salvaged by being torn apart, moved elsewhere, reassembled, and restored or modified for modern living. (See Fig. 1.) In other instances new houses have been built of salvaged materials—timbers, windows and doors, bricks, hardware, paneling, and so on—from a dozen other houses and as many areas. Some of these reproductions are so accurate in detail that it is impossible to tell from a brief study of the exterior whether the house was built yesterday or 250 years ago. The house shown in Fig. 2, built in modern times from old materials, is a good example. In many other instances we have to examine not only the structure (the roof in particular) but the floor plan as well, in order to arrive at a reliable conclusion regarding the various transformations a building may have undergone.

In beginning the study of house types for the two centuries prior to 1900, we need to start with a clear idea of the basic styles, and of their approximate dates of introduction into the country, and then to see how they spread as new territory was opened up to settlement. We shall examine each of these basic styles in turn. From that point on it will be easy to observe any variations in detail that

1. An original Cape Cod house being dismantled for removal to another site.

2. Central-chimney early American house, newly built from old material.

were introduced, to note how the styles overlapped as fashion (and social standing) took a hand in determining the kinds of houses people favored, and to distinguish the peculiar combinations that sometimes resulted from the scramble to stay in fashion without remodeling a house entirely.

The earliest Colonial houses were built by the English, the Dutch, the French, and the Spanish, with later contributions by Flemings, Swedes, Germans, Scots, the Irish, the Welsh, and others, so that in later years of the 17th and early 18th centuries there were many borrowings and adaptations; for example, houses originally of masonry were copied in wood, and vice versa. While farm and country houses were built by carpenters, to their own traditional ideas with perhaps local modifications,

the larger ones may have been close copies of foreign architectural styles, and may have had features the builders of smaller houses considered worth adopting. Then, with the opening of trails and roads, and the beginning of westward expansion, builders in one area copied ideas from another.

With increasing prosperity the earlier functional dwellings were dressed up, still without benefit of architects. Then came the books on carpentering and house design from England and Europe, providing descriptions and pictures of architectural treatments in vogue there; and suddenly the architects took over, setting the pace for the country craftsmen to follow. Academic architecture was launched with the adoption of Georgian styles in the early 18th century.

Beginnings

The early years of the 18th century therefore mark the beginning of American domestic architecture, for most of the houses built up to that time, though based on imported styles, had become adapted to the American climate, taste, and needs. To distinguish these houses from the more formal styles developed later, they are referred to simply as Early American—a term that covers a variety of Colonial types including the Cape Cod, the "saltbox," the one-and-a-half-, two, and two-and-a-half-story central-chimney houses of New England; the brick and wood "catslides" and the two-room plan, single- or twin-chimney houses of Virginia origin; the central-chimney Pennsylvania German; the end-chimney Dutch; and the two-room Swedish plan with its cater-cornered fireplaces. (See Fig. 3.)

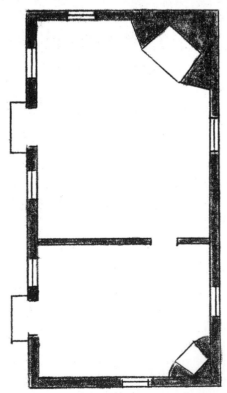

3. The earliest Swedish 2-room plan in America.

A number of these earlier styles retained their popularity, and continued to be built throughout the next century, but even those more recently built may have been altered almost beyond recognition. Window sizes and placement were changed, door side lights added, eaves extended; lean-tos, dormers, porches, porticoes, ells, and other appendages tacked on. In the 19th century fireplaces often gave way to stoves, and finally stoves to central heating. In New England, particularly, the huge chimneys remained only as deceptive ornaments, or were given thinner profiles that advertised the elimination of unneeded flues or the substitution of narrower ones to increase the draft called for by coal fuel.

The Georgian Era

In the 1720's mansions were being built throughout the original colonies in an imposing new architectural style called the Georgian. Very soon thereafter the availability of handbooks on house carpentry and architecture made it possible for the craftsman to construct smaller dwellings in the same style, in both brick and wood. An appealing feature of this style was the central hall (or passageway) made possible by locating a separate chimney in each gable or by centering them in the rear walls of the front rooms. This permitted not only a balanced façade but a more convenient arrangement of the floor space, even when the central hall became a large room.

The Georgian houses became more and more elaborate as time went on, some acquiring two pairs of chimneys and parapeted gables, or separate groups of chimneys on a hipped roof. By 1750 some Georgian brick houses had begun to acquire stone quoins at the corners, the wooden ones imitating stone by the use of vee-jointed wooden slabs. Dormers were fully pedimented, some arched and some, on the larger houses, with triangular and rounded pediments alternating. Inside, the hitherto paneled walls were reduced to dadoes with rich wallpapers above. Main doorways might be framed by side lights and pillared porticoes, with a Palladian window above replacing the earlier, flat-topped single or triple window.

Then, with the Revolution, came the Federal style which was merely a more austere form of the Georgian, one stripped of its ornamental features so that it became severely classical in feeling. This style was to persist for about forty years, when the Roman classicism gave way to the Hellenic, and the wholly American Greek Revival house became the rage. Soon almost every cottage had a pedimented gable housing the main entrance, if not a quartet of pillars or pilasters to give it the semblance of a Greek temple. It was at this point that many of the Early American houses were dressed up in imitation of this latest fad; gables were pedimented and corner pilasters applied, perhaps with running frets under the eaves, and over doors and windows —all to the confusion of old-house aficionados in the century to come.

Victorian Variety

Gradually the Greek Revival in its turn gave way to the Gothic Revival of the Early Victorian period, which saw a medley of adapted styles—Tudor, Roman, Italianate, French, and even Olde Englysshe—that lasted about thirty years. During this period, from 1833 on, the industrial age came into full flower, a period marked by degeneration of taste in architecture as the craftsman faded from the scene and the machine took over. The balloon frame made of two-by-fours largely supplanted the heavy timber frame, and

eventually "Steamboat Gothic", with its vertical siding and bracketed cornices, came to be regarded as the architectural triumph of the age. Unlike such contemporary innovations as Orson Fowler's octagonal house, it became popular wherever wooden villas were built.

The late Victorian houses, though often fussily ugly and ostentatiously ornate, were high-ceilinged and spacious, an advantage in a period when large families were the rule. This trend culminated, in the late 'nineties, in pretentious wooden houses replete with porches or piazzas, with wooden icicles or fretwork supported by flamboyant cut-out brackets, and with the inevitable iron deer on the lawn. Today many of these, stripped of some of their more garish elements, serve as comfortable homes, thanks to modern equipment and appliances.

This, then, is the mainstream of American architectural development over 200 years, though so brief an account does not do full justice to the contributions of several other nationalities, notably the Hudson Valley Hollanders, the Flemish, and the Pennsylvania "Dutch." The Swedes of Delaware apparently left no lasting mark on our domestic architecture, unless it is the single-story, high-roofed house with multiple dormers and corner fireplaces, and the characteristic steep, narrow gambrel roof that is unlike any other. The Dutch, on the other hand, were responsible for some notable stone houses with both gambrel and ridge roofs—but not for that sweeping Flemish overhang that for so many, mistakenly, is identified with the typical "Dutch" house. However, the value of such houses to us at the moment lies not in their original popularity but in the degree to which they were copied in succeeding decades by the pioneers and their descendants as they spread across the continent.

Most of the houses built as the West was being opened up were simplified reproductions of the major styles "back East." One notable exception to this rule occurred in the Ohio Western Reserve, claimed by Connecticut in 1799, where the Greek Revival house became for a while the ultimate in elegance. By 1850 the occupied territory extended beyond the Mississippi, touching the eastern fringes of Kansas, Texas, and Nebraska. Here, climate and geography as well as economic conditions influenced the domestic architecture, and the houses came more and more to reflect life as it was lived in these places, the style of each representing a distinct development of its own.

In Louisiana and the adjacent areas, the French influence made itself felt, and Spanish styles persisted for some time in Florida, in Texas and adjoining states, and in California, to be revived all over the country as the Victorian vogue came to an unlamented end.

With the coming of the railroads cheaper transportation made both ideas and materials available to all. Thus the lure of the local was gradually abandoned for the distant and the exotic. Soon, most styles of houses existing in the East were to be found throughout the continent. On the other hand, specialized types of dwellings were to become more and more in demand in the warmer climates and the flourishing coastal areas of the semi-tropical Southeast and Southwest. Even these underwent a process of evolution as time wore on, and it is highly probable that in the past hundred years many individual houses in these areas have become no longer recognizable for what they originally were. Of this much we can be sure: Some of the most desirable and admirable houses in America, in both appearance and suitability, were built 160 to 240 years ago, and they are still among the best in architecture that this country has to show!

Herein, then, lies the value of what follows: Knowing what the basic styles of American houses of 1700 to 1900 looked like and how they were built, we have a sound basis for analyzing old houses anywhere surviving to this day; we can see and compare the various pure styles, both inside and out, with examples that display the metamorphoses so many of them underwent—examples one may possibly encounter almost anywhere in the continental United States.

The following table gives the basic styles of old American houses and the periods in which they flourished:

Colonial (a) Late Colonial   —1700–1720
         (b) Early Georgian—1720–1760
         (c) Late Georgian —1760–1780
Post-Colonial
         (a) Federal   —1780–1820
         (b) Greek Revival —1820–1840
         (c) Early Victorian—1830–1850
         (d) Late Victorian —1850–1900

These dates are of course only approximations; during the period dealt with in these pages the various styles overlapped considerably.

4. Early Colonial.

5. Transitional Colonial.

6. Early Georgian.

7. Late Georgian.

8. Federal.

9. Greek Revival.

10. Transitional—Greek Revival to Victorian.

11. Victorian (Gothic Revival).

1

How American Styles Developed

Between the years 1700 and 1900 five basic American domestic architectural styles were developed: the Colonial, the Georgian, the Federal, the Greek Revival, and the Victorian. These terms, however, are not sufficiently precise to identify any particular type of house except in a general way. Colonial houses, for example, were not all of one style but fell into several categories, determined both by geography and by the origins of the settlers who devised them. The Colonial house of the Southern colonies was quite distinct from that of the New England area, and the "Dutch" Colonial differed from both.

From 1700 to 1800 Georgian houses changed completely so that we need to differentiate between Early and Late Georgian, as well as between Southern and Northern. The Federal style actually was a purely classical form of Georgian. Greek Revival, on the other hand, represented the first truly American architectural style, making use of Greek classical principles to interpret the new republican aspirations of the people. The chief characteristic of the Greek Revival buildings was

what Talbot Hamlin has called "an air of monumental permanence." In the hands of the small-house builder, however, it took only about forty years to run this idea into the ground, and reduce the farmhouse and cottage to pretentious absurdities.

Victorian actually was a mélange of styles, originally based on the medieval Gothic, developed by those who were tired of the classicism that had dominated American domestic architecture throughout the 18th century. Between 1830 and 1840, this development was given an extra fillip by the establishment of water-powered and, later, steam-powered sawmills and nail-making plants, which brought about a revolution in the structural design of houses. In place of the old-time heavy braced frame, the house could now be built of small-dimensioned lumber. Such a house was more flexible in design and simpler to construct and enlarge—and probably cheaper.

Victorian houses were thus freed of many design restrictions, and as time went on the designers and builders took more and more liberties with architectural style. Even Byzan-

12. Route over which spread architectural styles within, and from, the thirteen original states, Louisiana contributing the French influence, Florida and California the Spanish. Taken from a map dated 1855, and therefore omitting West Virginia.

tine and Egyptian influences can be seen in many of those that relied on the exotic for their appeal. With bandsaws and jigsaws that could quickly turn out fancy scrollwork, and, with machines that could carve a dozen wooden roses at a time, decoration almost did away with the need for careful design. And so Victorian styles ranged from the romantic to the ridiculous, and finally dug their own graves with their extravagances.

With these things in mind, then, we shall, in the following pages, trace in detail the identifying characteristics of the basic styles, and the effects of climate and national characteristics on the designs of houses and mansions in the expanding colonies and, eventually, in the thirteen original states. From these areas we shall follow briefly the expansion westward, and note how the basic styles were changed, modified, or superseded as settlers built their own homes based on designs with which they had been familiar "back East."

At the beginning of this expansion, in the early and mid-18th century, much of the migration actually took place between North and South, the later movement west being checked for a while by the French, who were establishing their own architectural styles in New Orleans and the Mississippi Valley. In Florida and California, at this time, the Spanish were putting up buildings (with the help of Indians, who added their own distinctive touch). Both of these architectural styles had their influence on future designs of houses, of which we are to take due notice here. Meanwhile we may note that:

The New England Colonial style was born in Massachusetts.
The Southern Colonial style originated in the Virginia colony.
Georgian first saw light in Pennsylvania, and so did Greek Revival.
Victorian evolved from the Gothic Revival simultaneously in both North and South.

With these things in mind, we can turn to the examination of the individual styles.

The Late Colonial House: New England

New England seems to have had a distinctive architecture all its own from the early days of the permanent settlements. Here, with some notable exceptions, the houses were predominantly of wood, with stone or brick chimneys, and stone cellars and foundation walls. Probably there were no more than a dozen masonry houses in New England before 1700.

Almost all Colonial houses built in New England before that date were severely plain and practical. What architectural value they had was largely due to their functional appearance plus their neat, compact proportions, and the natural beauty of weathered wood. By the 18th century most of the colonists were able to afford a little more than the bare necessities and so could indulge their fancy for more comfortable and attractive dwellings. At the same time new arrivals were bringing a knowledge of recent architectural developments in England, where the Jacobean styles had given way to the Stuart, and many ideas from the Renaissance architecture of the aristocracy had filtered down to the lower social levels. The Colonial craftsman was thus enabled to reproduce certain decorative details, especially of doors and windows, in order to give the Colonial dwellings a new look of importance.

The difference between the old façades and the new is well illustrated by a comparison of the Litchfield County (Connecticut) saltbox (1740; see Fig. 13) with the Selden house at Hadlyme, Connecticut (1780; see Fig 14). In the saltbox, window and door trim is plain and almost flush with the siding. In the Selden house the projection is greater and each window carries a moderately elaborate cornice, in addition to a dentilled main cornice, and quoins.

13. A New England saltbox of 1740.

14. Connecticut 2-story house of 1780.

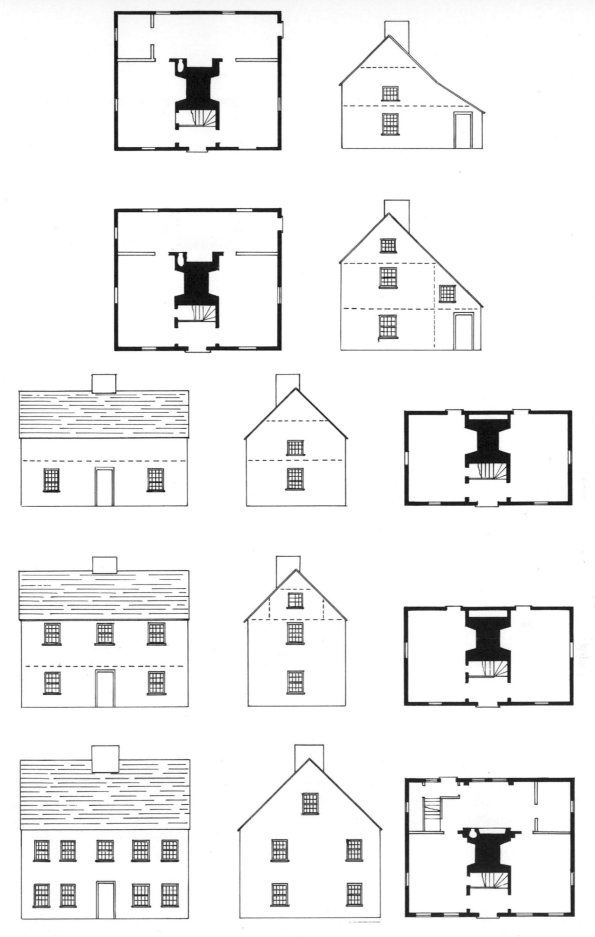

15. Drawings show basic plans for 1½-, 2- and 2½-story early American houses one and two rooms deep.

By the 1720 s, which saw more settled and prosperous times, larger houses began to be built, following the same old center-chimney plan, but often having more imposing entrances, with wider doors, (which were sometimes double), set off by pilasters and a pediment of the swan's-neck or scroll type, such as we find in some of the Deerfield houses and elsewhere. Thus, although the houses became larger, the ceilings higher, the windows bigger, and the façades—thanks largely to the addition of classical details—more imposing, the basic designs and floor plans as a rule remain recognizable as local developments from earlier prototypes. Many of the larger houses actually were more attractive and imposing in appearance without becoming truly classical in style. This was traditional architecture at its best!

From 1700 on, the traditional New England houses gradually came to include:

(a) The one-and-a-half and 2-story Colonial, one room or two rooms deep.

(b) The one-and-a-half-, two-, or two-and-a-half-story Colonial, one room deep with lean-to (the "saltbox").

(c) One story, two rooms deep (the Cape Cod).

(d) Two-story Colonial, one or two rooms deep, with framed overhang (the "garrison").

(e) The central-hall Colonial (transitional).

In addition there are the half-house, and the three-quarter house, having the entrance at or close to one end of the façade. These may be single-, one-and-a-half or two-story dwellings.

A basic feature of all these early traditional houses, the transitional varieties excepted, is the central chimney incorporating a fireplace for each room. Normally all such houses have whole or partial cellars, and the ridged roofs are without dormers, though the gambrel roof

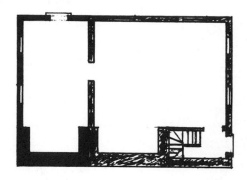

16. The Rhode Island stone-ender acquired its masonry gable wall through the addition of a kitchen lean-to fireplace alongside the living room fireplace, both utilizing one wide chimney stack.

is quite common on all except the saltbox. On some original saltbox houses, more rooms have been provided in the attic area by giving a gambrel form to the front of the roof, while retaining the plain lean-to roof at the rear. (See Fig 17). In the average New England gambrel (Fig. 18), the upper slope is not much shorter than the lower one, the lower slope being about 60 degrees from the horizontal—a feature especially common in Connecticut. But there are wide variations from this norm. For example, the 17th century houses of Massachusetts, which were mostly one room deep, have a much shorter upper slope (See Glossary), a characteristic they share with the gambrels of South Carolina, and in which they seem to follow the Swedish pattern, as will be shown later.

All of these houses, including many built up to around 1850, were of braced-frame construction. Such frames are of large timbers, tenoned together, with from eight to twelve posts supporting the structure. Neither the exterior walls nor the interior partitions were then required to carry any load. The drawing (Fig. 19) shows the main timbers of a typical two-story house, leaving out partitions and joists for clarity. Here it should be noted that in most of the New England states the sum-

17. Some saltboxes have gambrel-fronted roofs to increase space on second floor.

18. New England 2½-story gambrel.

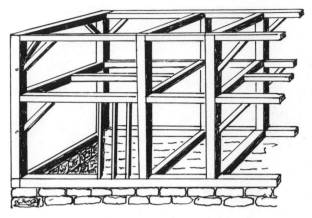

19. Detail of braced-frame construction.

mer beam runs from the gable end to the chimney. In Massachusetts houses, however, it runs from the front to the back of the house. External walls might be of either studs or planks. The stud wall might have been plain board, clapboard, or shake siding, applied over heavy sheathing board nailed horizontally to the studs, with lath and plaster on the inside except where boarding or paneling was used. The plank wall, consisting of thick boards running from sill to plate, could also be covered with siding on the outside and plastered on the inside.

Few early New England roofs had dormer windows, lights being placed in gables where necessary. Dormers added later often spoil the architectural effect of the compact, uncluttered New England house. Nevertheless, they were sometimes added as a simple means of increasing space as well as of providing light within the attics. An architecturally acceptable alternative on some early houses was to build wide "cross-gables" on the front of the roof to receive windows while adding to the usable floor space (See Fig. 155). Usually these gables were characteristic of houses built around 1700 or a little earlier.

To turn now to the particular kinds of houses: The typical New England two-story dwelling of the early 18th century would have a central chimney with a drip course, set well back on the ridge. A centered, simple door would be flanked by one or two pairs of small-paned windows in a balanced elevation. The trim would be plain, and the house would sit squarely on the ground. It would probably have transom lights above the door.

These are all original features of a New England house built around the turn of the 18th century. Not many such houses have survived unspoiled. For example, as we shall see later, many of them may have originally had but one window to each room, and that one extremely small. Today, such houses usually are found with pairs of larger windows. It is therefore evident that many of these houses have been carefully restored. Others have been changed in various other ways through the years, and the changes are seldom immediately apparent, a point that will be enlarged upon later. In yet other instances the changes are only too obvious, though not always to be condemned since they may lead to improvements in design, and may even represent steps in development from one type of house to another.

Such may or may not be the case with the Barnaby house of Freetown, Massachusetts, which was built before 1740. This is of a somewhat more advanced form than usual, the floor plan indicating that it has undergone many drastic changes. From the present plan it would appear that the chimney was originally in the east wall, since the chimney posts have later been doubled and an extra chimney girt installed. The chimney also has no fireplace on that side. Apparently, four rooms were added on the east side, together with a second chimney, providing three downstairs fireplaces. The location of the original side door is indicated at *B*, where a transom over the front door still remains. At any rate it is known that in 1914 two of the new rooms were cut off and the end wall rebuilt within

20. Barnaby house, Freetown, Massachusetts, built before 1740.

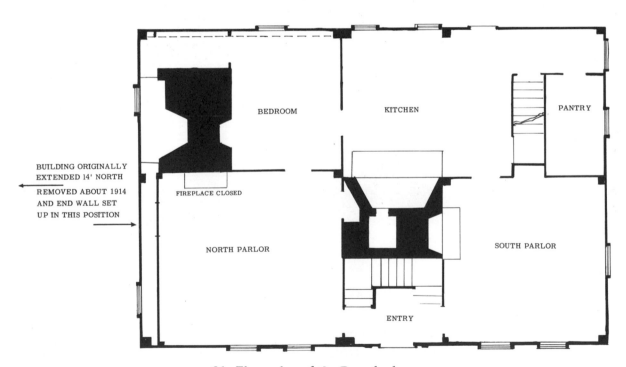

BUILDING ORIGINALLY
EXTENDED 14' NORTH
← REMOVED ABOUT 1914
AND END WALL SET
UP IN THIS POSITION

BEDROOM

KITCHEN

PANTRY

FIREPLACE CLOSED

NORTH PARLOR

SOUTH PARLOR

ENTRY

21. Floor plan of the Barnaby house.

nineteen inches of the new chimney. One fire-place also was closed off. So far as the façade is concerned, the house's architectural features are quite in keeping with the style of 1740. The double door with a bowed pediment and a six-light transom with fluted pilasters is far from classical, but highly decorative in a coun-try-carpenter fashion. The decorative window caps also add character. But from the photo-graph we see that the center chimney has been rebuilt without the drip course, a feature now rendered unnecessary by the modern flashing. The windows with the broad muntins appear to be original, and the house in its heyday

lonial house will have the second floor par-tially in the roof, so that the upper part of front and rear walls will be cut off by the sloping ceilings. (See Fig. 22.) All upstairs windows will then be in the gables. ("Eye-brow windows," which are long, low, and have a hinged sash at or near floor level, intro-duced in the 19th century, are discussed in the Greek Revival section.) In such a house the roof will come down to a level not more than four feet above the ceiling joists of the rooms below. If, however, the house has an original gambrel roof, the side walls of the house will go up no farther than the height

22. Typical 1½-story New England Colonial farmhouse.

must have been quite an imposing structure. No doubt the roof framing could tell a story in itself.

The One-and-a-half Story New England Colo-nial A one-and-a-half-story New England Co-

of the ground floor rooms. The need for more light and more space within the roof may necessitate the addition of dormers. That is why many of these one-and-a-half-story houses now have dormers added long after the house was built. The same cause lies behind the fact that many originally ridged-roofed houses had their roofs changed into gambrels, as did the one shown in Fig. 23. It is equally possible to encounter instances where a one-and-a-half-story gambrel has been changed over to a full two-story ridge-roofed house. In the instance of a plank house the change will be more evident in the attic, where the exterior planks will have been cut off to the gambrel shape.

The "Saltbox" The problem of increasing the space of the Early American house one room deep has existed in New England for as long as such houses have been built. The most practical method, and the most popular, judging by the number of "saltbox" houses in existence today, was by the addition of a single-story lean-to section at the back of the original one-and-a-half- or two-story structure. In later times such an addition formed a part of the original construction and the house was

actually built as a "saltbox", with the roof line unbroken from the ridge to the rear wall. This straight line, however, is in itself no definite proof that the lean-to was part of the original structure. With a house having a low main roof it would obviously be impossible to continue that roof line on down and still provide for a reasonably high rear wall (See Fig. 25.) The same problem would apply in the case of a taller house where the slope of the main roof was not flat enough to cover a deep main-floor room. In such instances, since the main roof could not be flattened sufficiently to permit a usefully high lean-to ceiling, the angle of the down-sweeping roof would have to be changed at the junction of the one-and-a-half- or two-story front section with the one-story lean-to. That this problem was common is evident from the number of saltbox houses having a broken roof line.

23. This 1½-story house was altered to gambrel.

24. The Deming House, Connecticut. Note break in roof line.

25. Modified saltbox with break in extension roof.

Where the house was built as a saltbox originally, the central chimney would have the largest fireplace at the back, with its flue incorporated into the main chimney structure. The chimney above the roof would then be rectangular. Where the lean-to was a later addition, a new fireplace would have to be built into or on to the chimney. This would mean the addition of a separate flue carried to the top of the main stack. The result would be a T-shaped chimney (clustered or pilastered), as seen in Fig. 26.

porated an enclosed rear stair to the upper floor. Since the upstairs space under the lean-to roof was usually of less than standing height, it served merely for storage, besides giving access to the two bedrooms from the rear. Often a few steps alongside the chimney would lead to the attic or open roof space. In rare instances a stair to the upper floor from the kitchen would call for a stair gable to give the necessary headroom . (See Fig. 27.)

The Cape Cod House The simplest of all New

26. Saltbox with T-shaped chimney resulting from added kitchen fireplace.

In practically all New England "saltbox" houses the rear lean-to section was divided into three rooms—a central kitchen with its huge fireplace; on one side of this (usually the warmer one) a bedroom reserved for childbirth (the "borning room"), and on the other a pantry or larder. Here also was incor-

England Colonial houses was the one-story, two-rooms-deep type with a massive ridge roof coming down to ceiling height. Originating in Massachusetts, this is known as the Cape Cod house, and in this area its prevalence is second only to that of the saltbox. It appears to be an 18th-century product, or at least to

27. A rear view of "Pond Bluff," South Carolina, to show the stair dormer made necessary by installing a staircase at the rear wall of a 1½-story house.

28. A typical Cape Cod house.

date no further back than the last quarter of the 17th century. This house, too, along with a central chimney has a centered door, with a room on either side. The 18th-century examples probably had the sash windows, then common, the upper sash of which was fixed,

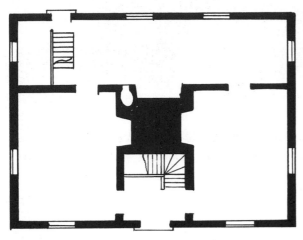

29. Floor plan of basic Cape Cod house.

the lower and smaller movable. Most of the earlier houses were built as single-story dwellings, the roof slope being quite flat for the expanse it had to cover. However, some seem to have been converted rather early to allow for sleeping quarters in the roof. A few of these houses acquire a little extra ceiling height upstairs by curving the rafters upward to form what is known as a "rainbow" roof. Cape Cod houses built at the turn of the 18th century might have a small gable window, but anything sizeable must be suspected of being a later "improvement."

The "Garrison Colonial" A 17th-century Colonial style having a framed overhang is included here because of its resurgence into popularity in modern times. This is the "Garrison Colonial," so called because of its resemblance to the very early combination frontier fort and dwelling which, besides being built of heavy timbers, had a substantial overhang to enable the defenders to fire upon

marauders close to the walls. The so-called "garrison house" had, however, an overhang of not more than two feet, and at the front only, and was actually copied from an Elizabethan style found in English towns. The word "garrison" nevertheless serves to define the style which was popular in the Connecticut River Valley and has become a favorite of builders and house owners in the mid- 20th century. Part of its charm doubtless is in the overhang itself, and part in the decorative pendant "drops" that usually, though not always, ornament the bottom ends of the upper story posts—or their present-day equivalents. (See Figs. 31 and 32.) These houses are usually two stories high, though some of the early ones consisted of a story and a half, and may have been either one or two rooms deep.

Partial Houses The "half house" and the "three-quarter house," are popular names for old houses, the first consisting of either a single room or a pair of rooms to one side of the chimney, and the second of a large room on one side of the chimney and a smaller room on the other. Many one-and-a-half- and two-story houses actually began life in this manner, and some were never completed. The procedure is made clear by the floor plans in Fig. 35. The changes that such a house can undergo by adding, enlarging, or taking away one room is well illustrated in the floor plan of the Barnaby house (Fig. 21). Typical half and three-quarter houses are shown in the photographs (Figs. 33 and 34). In some cases the extension of the front by adding a second room to one side of the chimney necessitated the provision of a second, smaller stack, as in Fig. 35. This is the plan of the Burnham-Marsh house in Wethersfield, Connecticut, which was built in 1740. It is of special interest because it not only shows one method of enlarging the house, but indicates how the central-chimney house could be de-

30. Cape Cod house with "rainbow" roof, a form of construction providing extra upstairs ceiling height.

31. A 17th-century garrison-style early Colonial house with its overhang pendills cut off, brackets and porch added, modern windows installed, and front door removed. The overhang, nevertheless, tells the story.

veloped into the central-hall plan that is the basic feature of the Georgian houses which were beginning to be built in New England at this time. In this instance, not only was an extra chimney added—along with an extra pair of rooms—but the former parlor fireplace was closed off and stairs were built into the wide hall thus formed. At the same time the old front door was sealed off and a new one which opened into the hall was added. This house was demolished, and other transitional ones are rare, but it sufficiently indicates a natural connection between the two kinds of plan, dating from the middle of the 18th century.* The advantages of this new room arrangement, even before the main stairs were made an important feature of the interior, were so obvious that the central-hall plan was quickly adopted for the two-story New England Colonial house. In most of these central-hall houses the old kitchen was moved to a rear ell, the rear room with which that ell connected then becoming a dining room.

Other, even more drastic methods were adopted for increasing the size of the original center-chimney house, for example that of building a one- or two-chimney section on to it. Sometimes this was accompanied by the removal of one or more of the original rooms —thus presenting even more of a puzzle today when it comes to determining the original plan. But unless the exterior also has been made over in a purely classical style, the twin-chimney house must still be classified as Colonial. Not until 1725 or later did what might be called academic architectural styles begin slowly to displace the traditional; yet even then, and long after, many of the Colonial styles continued to be preferred.

The Late Colonial House:
New York and New Jersey
(including Hudson Valley and Long Island)

Dutch settlements in the 17th century and later came to extend practically the whole length of the Hudson River, branching off along the Mohawk and into the Raritan. In northeastern New Jersey are houses erected by the French Huguenots; and in southern New York, Long Island, and northern New Jersey are the Flemish houses so often mistaken for the work of the Dutch.

Styles to be discussed here, then, include:

(a) Dutch Colonial
(b) Flemish Colonial
(c) French Huguenot Colonial

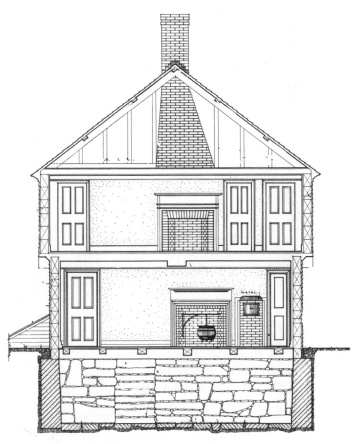

32. **Section through a late 17th-century Maine garrison house (restored). The squared log walls clearly show.**

---

* It is interesting to compare this plan with that of the Huguenot country house, "Fairfield" of Charleston, S.C. (Fig. 70).

33. Nantucket half house.

34. Nantucket three-quarter house.

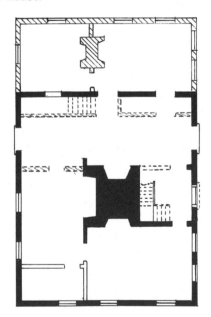

35. Floor plan of Burnham-Marsh house showing expansion to two-chimney house.

In northern New York State, where brick was more readily available than elsewhere, the Dutch built houses of this favorite material. The earliest of these were a story and a half high; later they were usually of two stories. In the former instance both the small Dutch bricks (1½x3x7") and the Dutch cross bond were used, the bond giving an interesting pattern to the walls. Later, under English influence, the larger English brick (2½x4x 8½") was adopted, together with the English bond. (See Glossary.)

By 1700 the old stepped gables had given way to roofs with a sloping gable. These were quite steep, with the coping of the gable walls extending a couple of inches above the roof. At the bottom of the slope the gable was squared off above the eaves. At the ridge the gables merged into the end chimneys, as can be seen in the picture of the Breese house at East Greenbush, built in 1732. These gable bricks are set in the famed Dutch "mousetooth" fashion—unfortunately not clear in the photograph.

In later brick houses the roofs were less steep, and therefore lower; and the gables were covered by the roof, which extended a few inches beyond the gable, the whole thing being finished off with a bargeboard.

The fact that the Dutch did not favor the gambrel roof does not mean that they were ignorant of it. It seems quite probable that they became acquainted with the gambrel through contact with the English colonists at the eastern end of Long Island, the Flemish at the western end, and the Huguenots in northern New Jersey. And it is certain that they used a form of gambrel roof on town

36. Breese house at East Green Bush, N. Y., shows a typical Hudson Valley Dutch brick house with steep roof.

37. The General Nicholas Herkimer house of Little Falls, New York (1754) sports a gambrel with unusually short sides. A heavy cornice gives it a classical air.

houses in New York City.

In the Breese house photo can also be seen the dagger-shaped anchor irons that hold the wooden frame to the masonry. The rear wall of this particular house, incidentally, is half-timbered. Here it should perhaps be mentioned that the Dutch version of the braced frame, used in both masonry and wooden houses, did away with the comparatively light joists customary in New England. Instead, beams spaced about four feet apart rested on the main timbers, and heavy planking was used for the floors. In many instances the ends of the upper floor beams were given additional support by curved brackets, which lent a decorative touch to the ground-floor interiors.

The only large two-story house in the Dutch style still standing in the Albany area

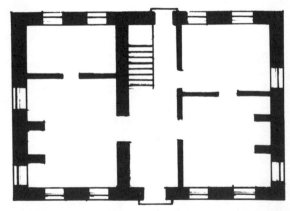

38. Floor plan of 4-room early Dutch Colonial house.

is "The Crailo" at Rensselaer (formerly Green Bush), New York. This is an L-shaped brick structure of small bricks laid in Dutch cross bond. The main section has a steep parapeted ridge roof with the customary end chimneys built into the gables. The ell portion, in contrast, has a gambrel roof with a pair of wide dormers. At present the main roof is covered in pantiles, the gambrel with shingles. On the main façade all the windows —nine of them, plus four in each gable—have flat arches, each with a projecting molded course over it. The lower windows have heavy cross-casings, the upper ones being simply divided vertically, and all of them, including the door transom, have diamond-shaped "leaded" lights. In addition there are two small attic windows, without mullions, in each gable. Between the windows on either side of the front entrance is a gun port, and there is a pair of circular lookouts in each of the upper gables. The ell of this building has modern sash windows and a transomed doorway and, except for the brickwork, seems to have little in common with the rest of the building. Built in 1642, "The Crailo" was added to and improved in 1762, 1790, and 1800. It has since been restored to its pre-

Revolutionary condition. Though inside "The Crailo" has little left of its original partitions, floor layout, or original woodwork, nevertheless the main fabric is of great historic interest as an example of the early Dutch house and frontier fort combined.

Farther down the Hudson, in Dutchess and Ulster counties, most of the Dutch houses were built of fieldstone. Moderately low roofs with clapboarded gables above the tie beam are also characteristic of these houses. Those built around the turn of the 18th century are generally one room deep, with two rooms in a row. There would be a fireplace in one gable, and a bed-place at the other end. Some had a cellar kitchen, others a lean-to kitchen either at the back or in a wing. Then, in the early 1700 s, the center-hall plan was introduced—a plan made possible by lengthening the house to accommodate a hall between the two rooms. Into this hall went the staircase, and at the same time shallow rooms were added to the rear of the building. These

39. The Crailo house at Rennsselaer, N. Y.

40. The finest Dutch Colonial house west of the Hudson—and also the oldest—is the Mabie home-stead at Rotterdam, New York, built in 1706. This is a 1½-story masonry structure built with-out mortar, "painted up" on the exterior, and plastered inside to the eaves, with the west gable clapboarded, the east gable of stone. Floors are planks on beams, with two rooms on each floor, two fireplaces, and an enclosed ladder stairway. The outbuilding, where slaves were housed, has one large room on each floor, and a basement fireplace.

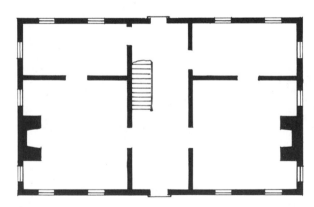

41. Floor plan of a later Dutch-style house with central hall.

two rear rooms, one on each side of the hall end with its rear door, had of necessity to remain unheated, the two fireplaces being located in the gable walls of the front rooms.

The Jean Hasbrouck house at New Paltz,

New York, was built in this period. Despite its large size it is gathered under one huge roof. The house is a story and a half high, with a granary above the upper floor. The walls are of rough, coursed stone, with the gable clapboarded above the tie beam. In spite of its location this is definitely a house of the Dutch style, put up by a Dutch builder for its Huguenot owner. Many other such houses have handsome Dutch (i.e., horizon-tally divided) doors surmounted by transoms, some with lights of tombstone shape and a finely molded hood. In the thick stone walls of some of these there may be stone arches over all openings, and solid, sheathed, or paneled shutters, depending on the date and quality of the construction.

In the 18th century, both the wood and masonry houses took to sash windows in place

42. Built between 1676 and 1695 of irregular ashlar, this stone house in the Dutch style was burned and later restored.

43. Among the interior restorations of the house were this mantel and tiled-cheek fireplace.

of casements, almost always with the two sashes equal in size. Because of the large size of the windows, 12-over-12 lights were quite common, and the upper sash, here as elsewhere, was generally fixed. The interiors of these houses were sheathed with wide boards, though the fireplace ends might have been paneled, and the fireplace masonry—facing and jambs—covered with Dutch tiles. In most of these houses the original open-fireplace hood of the 17th century was eliminated by building out jambs and chimney breast, with the addition of paneling and a bolection molding around the opening, and perhaps tiles covering the exposed brickwork and even the cheeks. The classical mantel and shelf came later. It was at this time that glass-fronted cupboards were built in the recesses when new fireplace walls replaced the hood, and paneled exterior doors were substituted for those of the earlier sheathed variety. After 1750 or so interior plastering became increasingly popular and, in the larger houses, the whitewashed ceilings disappeared from view.

Flemish Details In the 17th century in western Long Island and southern New York, and in the 18th century in northern New Jersey, it was the Flemish who shared with the French Huguenots a notable architectural triumph by introducing roofs with the now famous "Dutch kick." That appellation is therefore a misnomer, but one that it is going to be difficult to eliminate. In the beginning these flared eaves on gable roofs usually extended no more than a modest two feet from the house wall. By the middle of the 18th century they had become wide enough to call for posts to support the outer edge. In this way a useful porch became a feature of both stone and wood houses. But that was not the end. By the 18th century many of these houses had already adopted the wide gambrel roof that today we associate with New England. The combination of this roof with the flared overhang which the Flemish apparently developed, produced a new and highly attractive gambrel that ever since has been credited to the Dutch. (See Glossary).

This roof, with its short upper slope and long lower sweep, varies in proportion and angle of slope to accommodate both wide and tall houses. In every instance it provides for a full second story and often for a substantial garret as well. In all of the stone houses that can be classified as late Colonial, the gables were formed of wood siding. In the one-and-a-half-story versions of these houses shed dormers were sometimes used, as they were in the 17th-century Flemish gable roofs. On both kinds of roof, where dog-house dormers are found, they may be assumed to be late additions.

All these houses have end chimneys, which are always covered below the roof peak by the clapboard or shake siding. Usually, however, the fireplace backs were exposed, and through the back of the kitchen fireplace wall would protrude the rounded top of a large bake oven.

Some fine examples of the Flemish Colonial style in stone are still to be found in northern New Jersey. One of these is the Demarest house with a flared gable roof (Fig. 44), built around 1820 in regular coursed stone, with shingled gables. It has an unusual feature in the duplicate kitchens (one at each end), each of which originally had its own bake oven. The running shed dormer is of course a modern anachronism. The Ackerman house, which is somewhat earlier (1780), is of Jersey red sandstone, set in white lime mortar. The gables are shingled. In this house the chimney is inside the wall and the fireplace back does not show in the gable end. The roof overhang is about two feet, at both front and rear. The original windows were replaced around 1800.

The plan of this house (Fig. 47) is normal for its size and date, but the heavy wall separating the main room from the kitchen suggests that the latter was built on to the original typical Dutch center-hall house. Ordinarily, in such small Dutch houses, the rear (bed) rooms open into the front rooms so that no hall is needed except to accommodate a stair. A Dutch door at each end of the hall allows for additional light and ventilation on occasion.

Huguenot Variations The main difference between the plans of the Dutch and the Huguenot houses of northern New Jersey was that the shallow rear rooms of the latter occupied the full length of the rear wall; there was no hall to separate them. One notable exception, however, is the Lafayette house at Hawthorne, New Jersey, which incorporates a square stair hall into the center of the rear extension. These houses also had a separate outside entrance to each front room. Furthermore, when the one-and-a-half-story Huguenot house became too deep for a normal ridge roof, a gambrel was usually substituted. This would have the upper sections of the roof

44. The Demarest house, a stone Flemish Colonial of about 1820, considerably modernized.

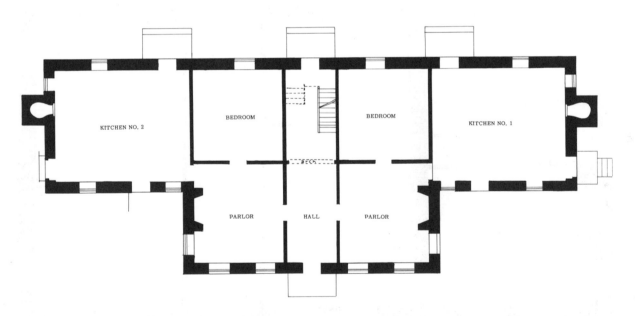

45. Floor plan of the Demarest house.

46. Modified Flemish Colonial house in New Jersey.

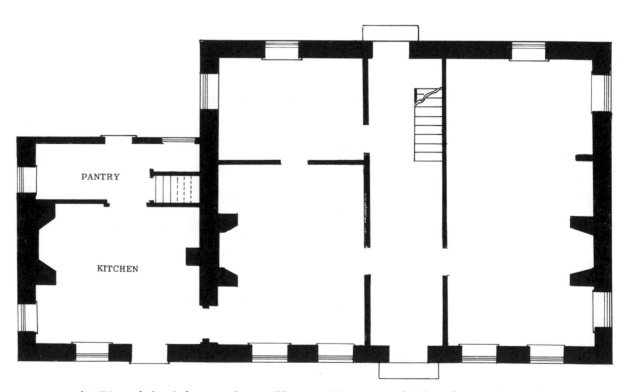

PANTRY

KITCHEN

47. Plan of the Ackerman house. Heavy wall separates kitchen from main section.

48. This unlikely-looking dwelling, badly in need of restoration, is the Lafayette house in New Jersey, a 2-room, 2-door Dutch-style house with a kitchen and dining wing added later, as the plan indicates.

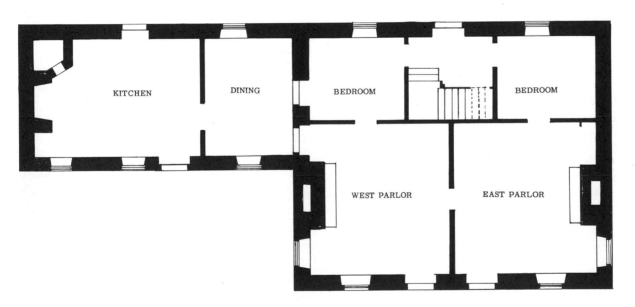

49. Plan of the Lafayette house, Hawthorne, N. J.

slightly overlapping the lower, while the bottom two or three rows of shingles would be given a slight upward tilt. Many of these houses, built in the early 1700s, had dormers, usually under a somewhat oversized, pedimented roof. With these may be contrasted the ridge-roof house which normally had a front overhang with the graceful tilt of the Flemish style. The simple plan of these houses was destined to be copied in many areas, so there must have been some advantage to it.

In western Long Island, where there was a mixed population of French, Flemings, Dutch, and Walloons, the houses were mostly of wood, but it is difficult to trace the influence of any one group on their structural features. Most of the houses had the flaring gabled roof, the earlier ones without supporting posts and the later and wider ones with them. Some of the houses eventually acquired a kitchen wing, either with the same flared roof or with perfectly straight overhanging eaves.

The Late Colonial: Middle Atlantic Colonies

In that large area covered by parts of western New Jersey, Pennsylvania, Delaware, and northern Maryland, English Quakers joined the Swedes, Finns, Scotch-Irish, Rhenish Germans, and Moravians in developing distinctive styles of Colonial architecture. In some instances the contributions of each colony are detectible in the surviving buildings to this day. Where this is not possible we may be reduced to accepting the old dictum that the Germans built their houses with central chimneys while the English kept their chimneys outside, and judge accordingly.

The Rhenish Germans and Moravians who settled in western Pennsylvania from 1710 on, built some medieval-style half-timbered houses, the heavy frames filled with brick nogging, which was sometimes covered with

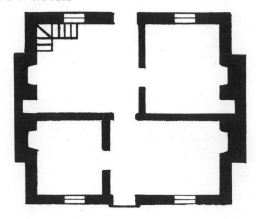

50. An early 4-room Maryland plan with chimney pents.

plaster. The only example still extant is the old Moravian meetinghouse at Oley Valley, which has been both a schoolhouse and a residence. This two-story structure was built in 1743 or thereabouts. Though there was a central chimney, the door was off center and the fenestration quite unbalanced, so the building has little architectural merit. There is a second small chimney at one end, probably added to accommodate stoves.

Even before this, however, the Pennsylvania "Dutch" (i.e. the Germans) were putting up houses of the Rhine Valley type with solid stone walls. These houses have a center chimney, with an enormous fireplace in the kitchen, which is the largest of the main-floor rooms. (See Fig. 51.) Since the chimney stack did not contain other fireplaces it did not need to be so massive as that of the New England Colonial house, even where the fireplace back was pierced to receive a stove pipe. Perhaps the commonest feature of these houses, and certainly the most striking, is the pent roof, destined to become an important characteristic of all such houses in this area.

The pent roof is a small, one-sided, continuous shed roof attached to the wall, usually at an upper-floor level. With both gambrel and a ridge roof there may also be a pent

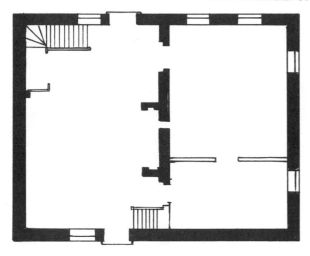

51. Rhenish plan of Pennsylvania "Dutch" house. Large fireplace is in the kitchen.

roof carried across the gable in line with the eaves. Where there was a first-floor pent roof, the door hood might consist of a pediment built into the front of it—a not very attractive innovation. With the gambrel there might also be a smaller pent roof carried across the gable at the junction of the two roof slopes. (See Fig. 53.) Such gambrel roofs were normally of a distinctively German variety with a definite overlapping break between the upper and lower slopes. The bottom edge of the lower section was also extended to form deep eaves in line with the outer edge of the pent roof.

Pent roofs were extremely common in lower New Jersey, where they sometimes extended not only the full length of the house

52. The Bonsall house, a Swedish log house in Darby, Pennsylvania, has the pent roof characteristic of homes in the area.

53. The Galloway house, built early in the 18th century, is a 1½-story Delaware brick.

but also across the gables. These New Jersey pent roofs are not, however, so spectacular as those of Pennsylvania, being finished off with a boxed cornice instead of with the deep coves typical of Philadelphia and Germantown.

Most of the pent-roofed houses had triangular gables to their steep roofs. The eaves molding might then be carried across the gables, to form a continuous drip course. Such roofs were often dressed up with tapered bargeboards, the narrower ends toward the top, presumably to improve the perspective. Hand-split shingles or plain, rectangular tiles covered the roofs. The tiles, held by projections on the back, were laid with the vertical joints continuous from ridge to eaves. The plain, central chimney of brick or stone would be topped off by a simple stone coping.

Other common features of western Penn-

sylvania stone houses are the use of quoins of either rough or dressed stone at the corners, the walls being of random-sized fieldstone, and the provision of a cantilevered door hood. Since the stone walls of these houses are often eighteen or more inches thick, the door reveals are quite deep, and therefore may be paneled. (See Fig. 56.) On the first floor the shutters are always solid, either paneled or plain, and carry hardware distinctive to this region. On upper floors they are more likely to be louvered.

The interiors of these houses also are interesting, the finish ranging from severe plastered walls to wood trim and paneling, with moldings cut into the solid pine and oak timbers. Partitions often took the place of walls—single boards with beaded or molded edges, held by simple strips at floor and ceiling. Ceilings, as elsewhere, ranged from

54. Dating from 1780, this Pennsylvania farm tenant house—called a "bank" house because it was built into a hillside—has a stone basement and one stone end. The rest of the structure is of brick, with a chimney at each end. The porch was an early innovation for Chester County. Rooms in this 14 x 33-foot house include a basement kitchen and one other small room; on the upper floor, two rooms at the left end with board partitions, and an 8-foot room at the other end. There is also a loft accessible by a gable stair. Two fireplaces occupy one chimney, stove flues the other—altogether an interesting survival with a Southern accent.

rough-hewn or molded beams and exposed planking to undecorated plaster. Most often the floors would be of random-width pine or oak planks, although there are occasional examples of walnut flooring, drilled and pegged. Since the windows are usually set well forward in the wall thickness, the inside reveals are quite deep. These in many instances are covered by wood panels, and many have a drawer built into the bottom of the recess. In the simpler buildings a candle shelf may sometimes be found over the inside door trim.

Not much can be said here about the larger houses of this area dating from the early 18th century. Almost all of them are far more Georgian than Colonial in style, and are accordingly to be discussed under that head.

In the Delaware Valley the Germans adopted features introduced by the Swedes. Notable among these were the two-room plan (Fig. 3) of the early log house—one small and one large room, each with a corner fireplace and an exterior door. More popular still was the three-room plan of two small chambers plus one large one with its corner fireplace against the interior partition. Such houses, 18 x 30 feet in size, were recommended by William Penn to the settlers. Houses of this plan were therefore at one time quite common from Pennsylvania to North Caro-

55. A typical Pennsylvania 2-story house of 1720, with a 1½-story kitchen wing added in 1798. This has a pent roof on the front only.

lina. Another mark of the Swede is the Swedish gambrel, a rather ugly but commodious style of roof, with short, almost vertical sides and a very low-pitched upper section (See Glossary.)

"Log" houses built by the Swedes were made of planks; these in more recent times have been covered over with clapboards so that they are hard to detect. They are mentioned here because of later references to this same style in the Middle West. The timber-framed houses of the Swedes used beams instead of joists in the same manner as that of the Dutch in New Jersey. It was the Swedes who originated the corner fireplace which may be placed either across a corner angle or parallel to one of the walls.

Probably the most famous example of the Swedish three-room plan adapted to a city dwelling, and still in existence, is the Letitia Street house, moved to Fairmount Park from downtown Philadelphia. This is a brick structure built around 1714, using Flemish bond, with one large and one somewhat smaller room on the main floor. Its sills are approximately level with the ground. The larger front room has a centered door flanked by a pair of sash windows with paneled shutters. Over the door is a flat bracketed hood, and above are three windows to balance the openings below. The rear wall has the same door and window arrangement. In the right-hand wall are two windows, one to each downstairs room, and a similar pair for the rooms above. In addition there is a small window in the gable, and in later times a shed dormer has been added. The eaves are supported by the usual deep cove molding. Inside, the room partition has a center door, with the fireplaces on one wall and a sheathed-in staircase on

56. Pennsylvania cantilevered hood is panelled, as are the door and the recess in the stone wall.

57. The only surviving Dutch-style house in Delaware—a center-chimney, 1½-story cottage with front roof overhang, its trim similar to that of the Hudson Valley houses.

the other. The trim is confined to an oversized bolection molding around each fireplace, supporting a corniced mantel.

In its balanced façade and trim this house is reminiscent of the early Georgian—which is not surprising, since most of the Pennsylvania houses of that period were built by English settlers fresh from Georgian England. Interior trim and other details appear to be additions made a quarter of a century later.

The Late Colonial: Southern

By 1700 the typical Virginia small-house plan had developed from the primitive one-room to the two-room, either with or without a central hall. These houses, whether brick or frame, had a chimney at each end,

sometimes projecting from the gable wall, sometimes built flush with it. At this period, also, these houses were enlarged by adding small, single-story rooms to the backs of the two-room, story-and-a-half or two-story houses. This practice resulted in a roof whose shape was similar to that of the New England saltbox, but which in the South is called a "catslide." The plan of the catslide house likewise was a traditional one antedating the central-hall units one or two rooms deep.

Since this original colony was settled by aristocrats and people of wealth, the plan of very many Virginia houses was that of a mansion—with kitchens and servants' quarters separate. The simplest such plan would then be a central-hall unit with a closed entrance porch giving access to the hall. These houses

58. "Hager's Fancy" at Hagerstown, Maryland is a 2½-story fieldstone frontier dwelling built in 1740, over two free-flowing springs. It has a central brick chimney, with the entrance to one side. This enables one chimney to take care of three fireplaces, reversing the arrangement of the early Swedish 3-room plan.

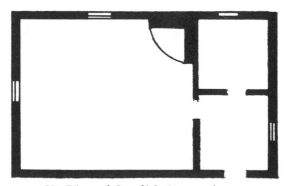

59. Plan of Swedish 3-room house.

were usually a story and a half high, though two- and two-and-a-half-story examples are occasionally found. Important aims in their design are good air circulation and reduction of heat from the kitchen chimneys. In an endeavor to maintain such advantages while adding more rooms, several standard plans were developed for the larger houses—the T, H, L, and U shapes. The T-plan was formed by adding a central rear extension, with its own fireplace and arches or door openings on each side for ventilation. In Maryland the T-plan might be translated as in Fig. 67. Here, the stair is removed from the central

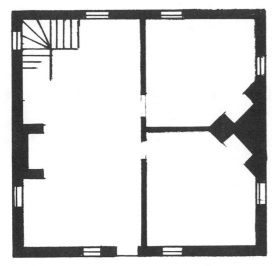

60. Floor plan of a typical Quaker house.

62. Floor plan of the Letitia Street house.

61. Letitia Street house, c. 1703–1715, the most famous house of the Swedish 3-room plan.

63. The Woolman house is a rural New Jersey adaptation, in brick, of the early Swedish plan. This plan should be compared with that of the much earlier Letitia Street house. The Woolman house is much more nearly square (18′ 6″ x 26′ 6″) but requires two corner chimneys to the other's one. In one corner of the larger room a stair winds up to the second floor. Today the house has a substantial three-pillared porch and a large wooden lean-to addition. Otherwise it is still a good example of West Jersey country architecture of the late 18th century.

hall to the extension. In Tennessee the arrangement might be as in Fig. 71. Next in popularity was the L-plan. Variations of this ranged from the Pennsylvania Quaker plan with a wing (Fig. 68) to the house with three rooms and a hall in line. The house of Sir William Berkeley with its one-room ell (Fig. 69) is a good example.

In South Carolina the houses more often followed a rectangular plan, two rooms deep, with chimneys in the longitudinal walls. Similar central-hall plans in Virginia occasionally have the end chimneys arranged to serve two fireplaces each, the fireplaces being set at an angle in the four adjacent corners of the two end rooms. (See Fig. 72.)

Besides the large plantation houses, there were many smaller residences erected in the 18th century by settlers throughout this area. Most of the houses after 1725 were two rooms deep, with two or four chimneys. Both in Virginia and in North Carolina gambrels were popular, some of those in Virginia having hipped gables. The similarity between Virginia houses and those of New England is striking—the Nicholson house at Williamsburg is a good example. In North Carolina, however, gambrel houses one room deep almost always have a lean-to at the rear and a shed-type porch at the front as in the Booth house at Edenton (see Fig. 75). Differences between these two include the fact that the Williamsburg house is set up on a high foundation and has the chimneys built flush with

64. Down in Mississippi is the Evans-Wall house (late 18th century), somewhat similar in arrangement to the Pennsylvania example (see Fig. 54) but of wood, with a sheet-iron roof that must have been like a stove-plate in summers. Here are the Virginia-type end chimneys, the high basement, and the full-length porch with its double stairs to the ground—a typical plantation-style building with wide, flaring eaves.

the gables. In the North Carolina house the chimneys are outside and spaced away from the gables, supposedly to reduce the heating effect in the upper rooms. This house also has shed dormers as opposed to the pedimented style—a feature which suggests a Huguenot influence.

In order to understand some of the variations and similarities in the styles favored in these Southern areas, we need to know by whom they were settled. Various national groups with differing building traditions moved south as trails were opened, and came in to coastal settlements from the West Indies, or from other parts of the South. North Carolina, above Albemarle Sound, was first settled by Virginians. Huguenots founded

Bath; another group, together with Germans and Swiss, built New Bern. In South Carolina, Barbadians called their settlement Albemarle Point. Others, together with French Protestants from England, founded Charleston. Germans and Scotsmen were the first settlers in Georgia. Immigrants, coming in through Philadelphia from European Protestant countries, filtered down via Virginia into the Carolinas and to Georgia. In the 18th century, as travel became easier, native-born emigrants from the Northern states joined this movement, bringing still other ideas with them. In Colonial days, therefore, these various ideas and methods were bit by bit adapted to climate and terrain and to the economic conditions of the settlers, and the

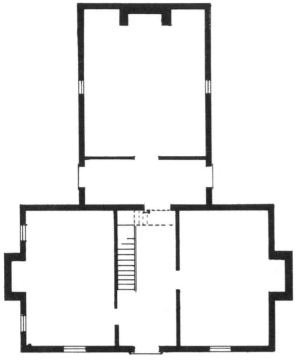

65. Floor plan of Virginia T-shaped house.

local styles evolved. In this way the tropical piazza, the jerkin-head roof; a modified Quaker plan, the hipped gambrel, and similar innovations eventually became architectural hallmarks of the Southern states.

In examining the characteristic features of Southern Colonial houses, we shall encounter these and other features peculiar to certain areas, and be able to compare them and to trace their origins. For example, while the French Huguenots livened the streets of Charleston by painting their stucco houses in bright colors, the West Indians solved for the Charlestonians the problem of keeping cool in hot weather. The idea of the piazza was imported from the Caribbean islands, as was the custom of arranging the house rooms in a line to secure cross-ventilation, with the gable to the street and a pleasant open garden to look out upon from the piazza's shade. This, combined with the fact that Charleston is relatively free from malarial mosquitoes, and enjoys sea breezes in the summer, made

66. "Otwell", Maryland, is an excellent example of the T-plan house, with a typical Maryland gambrel. The original brick building is dated around 1670.

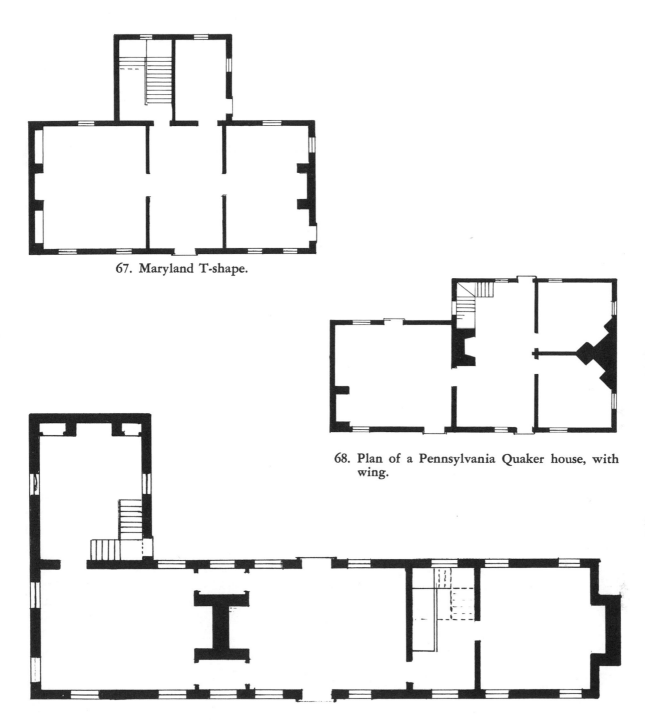

67. Maryland T-shape.

68. Plan of a Pennsylvania Quaker house, with wing.

69. Virginia L-shaped.

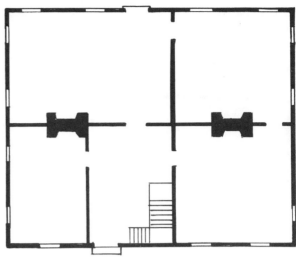

70. A South Carolina plan.

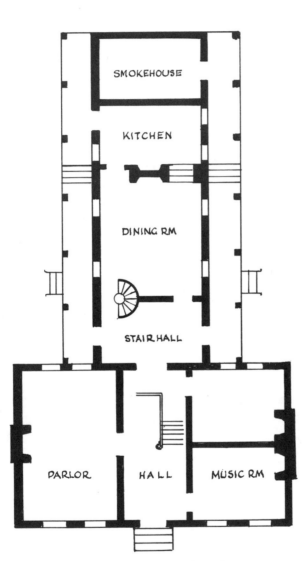

71. Tennessee L-shaped.

the town the most popular resort for heat-stricken planters and their families.

It was in South Carolina, too, that the typical plan for riverside plantation houses was developed. Through roads were few, and it became as necessary to have a main entrance to the house on the land side as it was to have one facing the water—that much-used highway between plantations for both social and business affairs.

In Fig. 77 is the original plan of the ideal house for such a purpose, developed by the Dutchman Jan Van Arrsens, who built it in 1686. A similar public benefactor was Benjamin Simons, a Huguenot, who devised what was to become the standard plan for the Charleston house. (See Figs. 78 & 79.) Here three rooms in single file encourage cross-ventilation while providing shade for the walls, by means of the piazzas along both

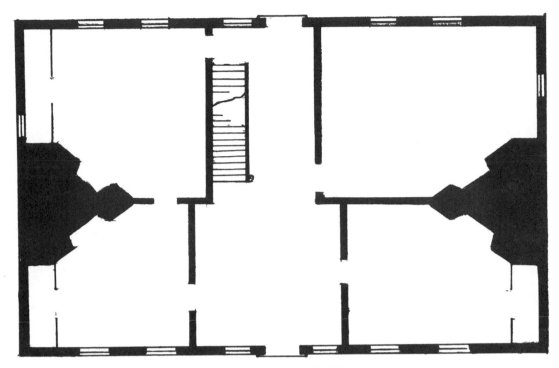

72. Virginia central hall plan.

73. "Hanover," in South Carolina, is an interesting hybrid—a 1½-story Huguenot house of 1720 with a distinctive gambrel roof having an almost flat top section, pedimented dormers, and external end chimneys, unusual in this state. The chimneys are pilastered to accommodate upstairs fireplaces. Note also the tall main-floor windows and low door, once covered by a full porch which also hid the high foundation.

74. The Nicholson house at Williamsburg, a traditional gambrel two rooms deep.

sides. The main walls were clapboarded outside, plastered within. The partitions were of vertical boarding; the frame of heavy posts and beams under a hipped roof. Two fireplaces, back to back, take care of the winter heating; two more on a smaller separate chimney confine the cooking to a smaller room, located beyond the stairs and to a dining room with built-in corner cupboards.

Because of these and similar foreign contributions to Southern architecture it is both interesting and instructive to compare houses of this variety with their counterparts in the North, where foreign elements have also contributed their share of ideas in developing the most desirable kind of dwelling.

75. The Booth house at Edenton, N. C.—gambrel over single file of rooms.

76. "Sweet Hall," Virginia, is a 1½-story brick house dated about 1700. The steep roof forms Dutch-style gables, and the decorative pilastered chimneys are almost Jacobean in feeling. The bricks are set in English bond, with a stuccoed front and molded water table. Under the porch (a later addition) the façade is nicely balanced, with five tall dormers over the doors and windows, a dentilled cornice tying the whole together. As a whole, "Sweet Hall" is a fascinating link between the medieval and the Georgian.

77. The Jan Van Arrsens house of 1686, exemplifies an original plantation style designed to face both river and land approaches.

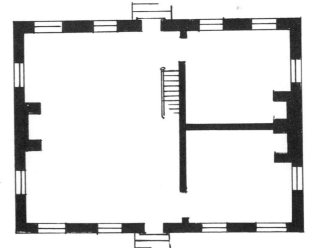

78. "Middleburg," a Huguenot plantation house, is the oldest dwelling in South Carolina (1699). This single line of rooms with flanking piazzas became the basic plan of the Charleston single house.

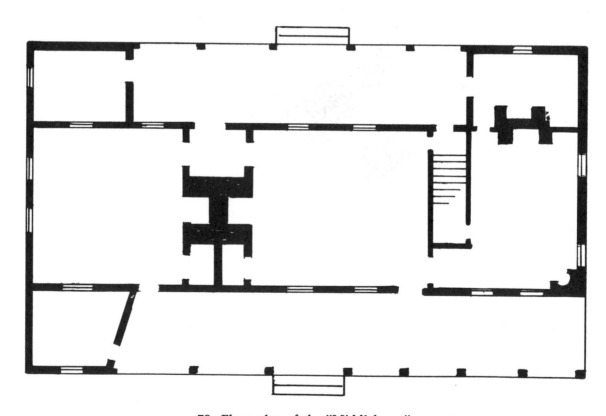

79. Floor plan of the "Middleburg."

2

The Georgian House 1725-1780

The Georgian house on its high foundation, with its imposing entrance and well-
balanced exterior, was the embodiment of
genteel formality. The principal features of
such a house were the wide, paneled door
with a row of rectangular lights either in the
door itself or in a transom over it. There
might be a window at one or both sides of
a door, but not yet as a part of its framing.
The doorway might be flanked by plain or
fluted pilasters. Above the door a round-
topped window might light the landing. Elsewhere, windows would be of the modern
sash type, counterweighted, and having from
18 to 24 panes. They would be framed by
an architrave with, perhaps, a small, flat cornice, triangular pediments being reserved for
the more pretentious houses. Crowning all
this would be the roof—low-gabled to permit
of a well-proportioned classic pediment, or
a gambrel (despite the fact that gambrels
have little classical "feel"), or even a hipped
roof. A classic cornice would replace the traditional eaves. Dormers, if any, would be

narrow, with a triangular pediment. Sometimes the roof ridge would be flattened to
form a deck enclosed by a balustrade. The
Georgian chimney would be plain, or (occasionally) supplied with a modest cap.

The Georgian Interior

Inside the Georgian house the keynote is
still the use of classic forms, rich and often
elaborate in both surface finish and work-
manship. Beyond the entrance hall with its
high ceiling would be a handsome staircase
with a decorated open string, and three turned
or twisted balusters to the step, each different because of the varying lengths. A molded
and polished mahogany handrail would sweep
gracefully into a turned or carved newel post.
At the other end of the treads, the stair wall
would be paneled to the height of the handrail.

Most of the rooms would be paneled—
sometimes merely the chimney wall, or per-

65

80. The Trent house in New Jersey, one of the finest examples of the traditional style in this area, has Swedish features including corner fireplaces and a fine staircase in a wing off the stair hall.

haps the two interior walls, with the rest papered or painted. All floors would be of hard wood, perhaps parquet, or painted with decorative borders and centerpiece. Doors and windows alike would be framed in a simple architrave, often with ears (crossettes). Cornices were rare in these earlier years, but paneled interior shutters might be found. Fireplaces would be smaller than those of the Colonial type, and the rectangular opening would be faced with marble or tile. The overmantel would consist of a large panel with an eared architrave and a broken triangular or scroll pediment: all very formal, with a touch of the baroque, and very beautiful in a robust sort of way. But Georgian was a living style, and around mid-century important changes were to be noted.

Later Georgian

In its stately march toward maturity, the Georgian house became even more imposing. The doorways were flanked by pilasters or engaged columns, with either a cornice or a pediment—perhaps the elaborate swan-necked type with rosettes, and possibly a central ornament such as that popular symbol of hospitality, the pineapple. Semicircular fanlights, too, became the vogue, and louvered blinds at the windows. The second-floor hall would now have a triple-sashed Palladian window.

The more pretentious residence would by now have acquired a central projecting pavilion with a pedimented gable, to house both door and window. Otherwise pilasters might reach the full height of the wall, each with its own architrave and frieze nestling under the house cornice, which completed the architectural order. Both of these arrangements had the advantage of permitting the second-floor windows to be of full height. In houses

81. This wooden Georgian house is transitional in style, with end chimneys, decorative fanlight, and plain trim including door pediment and pilasters, but a low foundation.

of three stories or more—and many such were built—the height of the uppermost floor was of much less consequence.

Masonry walls now acquired quoins to add weight and solidity. On wooden houses these quoins would be copied with grooved planks; on brick houses, either stone or grooved stucco would serve. Roof decks soon became *de rigueur*, often with a Chinese lattice rail; and the dormers would be capped by alternating segmental and triangular heads.

to be framed with carved trim and a garlanded frieze, plus a console-supported shelf. Wood cornices were applied to the ceilings, elaborate carvings to stair rails, balusters, and newels. And so it went: more detail but less robustness; more ornament but also more delicacy as the Adam influence made itself felt, and as the Georgian slowly declined into the austere Federal style with its attentuated Doric porches, exquisite Adam trim, and oval rooms.

Late Interiors

The interiors of these later Georgian houses followed much the same pattern as the exteriors, with pilasters flanking doors and chimney breasts, the doors acquiring a frieze and cornice or a pediment. Cupboard doors were likely to be arched, and fireplaces

Georgian in New England

The difference between the later traditional architecture of New England and the Georgian is the difference between folk art and classical design. The Georgian had to be symmetrical, its façade balanced, a requirement that took precedence over interior arrange-

82. "Woodford" in Philadelphia is of special interest because of the full entablature that is carried right around the house at second-floor level. This forms part of the doorhead, with a pediment above it. On the second floor is a Palladian window with another pediment above it, the total effect being that of one house surmounting another. This is an L-plan house of 1750.

ment. The style followed the rules of classical design current during the Renaissance; it was geometrical, with no allowance for the accidental that is part of the charm of evolutionary development. This is perhaps one reason why the classical styles of architecture came late to New England, so that few true Georgian houses were built before the later 1700s.

This area, with so many fine and beautiful houses in the traditional style to its credit, was slow to accept the formal architecture based on the English style of the late Stuart period with academic Palladian overtones. The tendency was rather to stick to the older building types and structural features, adding only such decorative architectural embellishments as seemed desirable. With the adop-

tion of the central-hall plan—which came as a natural development in masonry houses—the traditional houses became much more convenient as well as imposing, even though there were but four or perhaps five rooms on the main floor.

By 1725 a great many of these later New England houses were a full two stories in height, and the front and rear rooms were of equal size. The roof ridge therefore marked the center line along which the longitudinal room partitions were arranged. In wooden houses the two chimneys were located in these partitions, with a fireplace in each room. In houses built of brick, or wooden houses having brick end walls, the natural thing was to make the chimneys a part of the brick wall and so save construction costs. The simplest method here was to have but one chimney per gable end, with fireplaces in two adjacent room corners. Some owners, however, preferred to build two separate stacks, and to center the fireplaces in the end walls. This was more often done in the larger houses, which were then made more imposing in appearance by extending the brick gable upward to form a parapet joining the two stacks above the roof ridge.

Such houses, having moved the kitchen into an ell, obviously had many of the conveniences of the formal Georgian floor plan, though they were far from classical in design or appearance. They were rarely symmetrical, their ceilings were low, and they still hugged the ground in the manner of the other late Colonial houses. Nevertheless, many of them were given a classical "feel" by the installation of pilasters and pediments and cornices, the application of moldings to doors and windows, and so on.

Those who, at this early date, fancied the academic Georgian that was making its appearance elsewhere, were often faced with the problem of translating into wood a style that

83. The Read house of Newcastle, Delaware is almost Federal in character with its late semicir-cular-topped doorway, Palladian window, decorative lintels, classical dormers, and twin chimneys with parapets and roof balustrade.

owed much of its success to the use of stone or brick. In one instance the owner of a brick house saved himself considerable expense by covering the entire brick front with wood and creating a classical façade in that easily worked and far less costly material. However, in spite of such early indifference, the Georgian house began to receive serious attention within the next two decades or so. In particular it appealed to the newly fledged shipping magnates of the seaport towns, where overseas trading gleaned the first great fortunes.

By this time American architects had plenty of examples in England to use for models. Furthermore, thanks to the availability of books on architecture, carpenters' guides, and so on, the American builder was able to familiarize himself with the details of the new style, and to adapt them to the smaller house, leaving the mansions to the trained architects. The result has been that today we have a large number of well-designed, well-built, medium-sized early Georgian houses for study —houses of thoroughly classical design adapted both to the New England climate and to the special requirements of the original owners.

Southern and Middle Colony Georgian

Regional differences in the Georgian style were apparently far fewer than the differences in the earlier styles of architecture. Most of these variations in Georgian plan and detail rose out of the climate and conditions of living. For example, the larger Southern house did not have to accommodate either kitchen or servants, both of these be-

84. "Mount Lubentia," a Maryland house built in 1770, features exceptionally fine late Georgian trim, of which this attractive cupboard is a sample.

ing in separate buildings. This fact permitted free use of the main floor for social and family purposes, making possible great symmetry of plan to match the balanced exterior. The designer did not always make use of this advantage, however. In such great Georgian houses as "Westover" in Virginia, the rooms have little relation to the building axis, or to the main entrance to the hall.

Some of the principal differences between the New England houses and those of the rest of the colonies can be summarized as follows: In the South, where the early Georgian houses appeared about twenty-five years before they did in New England—as did hipped and jerkin-head roofs—two-story porticoes were favored. The middle colonies went in for paneled shutters, while Philadelphia

and Charleston shared a predilection for stucco over brick and stone. In some important Southern mansions, the post-Revolutionary trend toward plain plaster walls and delicate plaster ornaments of the Adam style came early. In the smaller houses of Virginia, ashlar and cut stone were often used to great effect. Such houses largely followed the central-hall, four-room plan, though some located the hall in one corner so that it gives direct access to all three rooms in the other corners.

As far as the interiors are concerned, the tendency after 1750 was to substitute low dadoes, with decorated plaster walls and ceilings, plus architectural trim for the fireplaces, doors, and windows in place of the earlier room-high paneling. Some of the small houses successfully achieved high architectural qual-

85. "Mount Pleasant," in Philadelphia, one of the North's finest Colonial houses, boasts this beautiful staircase in a lateral hall off the main hall. It dates back to 1770.

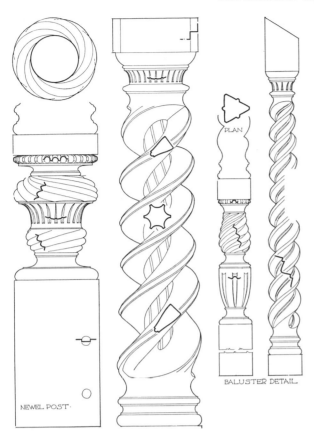

87. The Seavey house, Rye, New Hampshire: a plain exterior with a splendid interior.

low gable sheathed in vertical boarding so that it forms a smooth pediment, effective in contrast to the clapboarding beneath. Over the main entrance below is a porch consisting of a dentilled pedimented roof supported on slightly tapered square pillars, the pilasters behind them being fluted. There is evidence,

86. Typical examples of late Georgian decorative woodwork in New England mansions.

ity by means of such devices as dark stone quoins, string-courses, and window facings against a background of white stucco.

One of the most attractive of the smaller houses, with a far different appearance and arrangement than the typical one just described, is the James Semple (or Randolph-Semple) house (Fig. 96) at Williamsburg. This is a five-room house built in 1780. It consists of a two-story central unit flanked by single-story wings. The main unit contains a ground-floor salon with fireplace, and two small chambers above. These chambers are reached by a winding stair located behind the chimney in the left wing. In the wings are a dining room and a drawing room, each with its own fireplace. The central roof is a

88. Transformations from traditional to Georgian sometimes began with the interiors, as these photographs show.

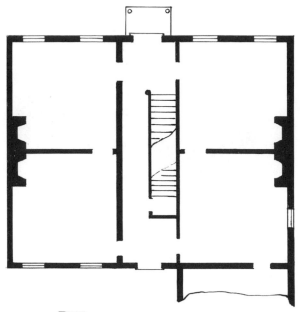

89. Plan of typical Georgian house with end chimneys.

however, that the pillars were once slender Doric columns.

The Georgian houses of Charleston had little in common with those of Virginia. Mellow brick and tinted stucco, red tiles, and graceful wrought-iron balcony rails and gates gave the streets of the South Carolina city an exotic air. Most of the house lots were narrow though deep, and the long, shallow "single" houses were designed to take advantage of this fact. This single file of rooms presents its gable end to the street, the main part of the house consisting of a reception room, hall, and dining room. On the street façade were three windows, with a door at one side leading to a long piazza. Off the piazza was a door leading to the entrance hall. Since the reception room was much larger than the dining room—the former having three windows and the latter two—the hall door was several feet off center.

Beyond the dining room, the offices and

90. The Richard Derby house in Salem is 2½-story brick, gambrel-roofed New England Georgian, built in 1762. Note the rusticated door jambs with fluted pilasters superimposed, the arched windows, and the corner windows in the gable end.

91. The stone façade of this house, "The Lindens" in Danvers, Massachusetts, was covered with wood to permit the addition of Georgian detail at lower cost. Note the attached Corinthian columns, the clapboard end, and the stone kitchen wing.

kitchen were in a narrow wing. With this arrangement, each of the rooms overlooked the garden, and each had available through ventilation. Still farther down the line, in a structure separated from the main building by a strip of garden, were the servants' quarters.

In contrast with this was the square house which is simply one with a center-hall, four-room plan, having fireplaces centered in the pairs of rooms and offering a minimum of interference to the summer breezes. In this respect both houses benefited from high foundation walls and very high ceilings. As a result the second floors in each instance are the coolest in hot weather and therefore contain the most-used rooms.

In North Carolina a great many of the early houses were destroyed in the Tuscarora War of 1713. As a result, in the rebuilding a good many of the new settlers brought their own styles with them. To the Moravians are owed the houses with German characteristics; from South Carolina come the sheltering piazzas. Maryland and New Jersey introduced their own varieties of patterned brickwork; and in the Tidewater areas Virginia styles were copied, while New Bern acquired Hudson River mansions and elaborate Pennsylvania parlors. As a result of all this no distinct regional style was developed.

An excellent example of such extraneous influences is the cupola house at Edenton (Fig. 101). Here we have a New England

92. One of the less ornate of "The Lindens" ' fireplaces in the Adam manner, with French tile facing and tiled hearth.

overhang with brackets, beaded clapboards, and a steep roof, while the second chimney has sloping offsets and in the cross-gable there is a rare oval window—all features apparently of Virginia origin. Built in 1715, this house was remodeled in 1758, when interior panelling, sash windows, and the cupola—all Georgian features—were added. The house is therefore an interesting example of a transition style between traditional and Georgian.

Georgian into Federal

In the years immediately prior to the Revolution the Georgian exterior gradually became more severely classical, though its severity and purity were made up for by lavish decoration of the interior in the Roman manner. In New England, where wood was still the favored building material for houses, a more intensely classical effect was secured by the use of flush boarding, stucco, or painted brick for the exterior walls. Where an effect of compact solidity was secured by hiding the roof behind a balustrade or parapet, the same effect was softened by the employment of curved forms, without any loss of simplicity. Doorways acquired elliptical fanlights, later widened to cover flanking windows; projecting rear bays became curvilinear. Inside rooms were rounded or elliptical, and the interiors were delicately decorated in low relief in the Adam manner. Because the architects now had a wide choice of models to follow (the excavations of Herculaneum and Pompeii having exposed earlier fallacies about the rigidity of classical design) they had much more freedom to experiment.

One of the finest and largest of these post-Revolutionary houses in brick is the three-story John Brown residence (Fig. 104) erected in 1786 at Providence, Rhode Island. It has the characteristic narrow pedimented pavilion, an elaborate Palladian window in an arched recess over a fine Doric entrance porch of wood. This house is noted for its unusually rich interior details, especially the baroque ornamentation of the stair, doorways, overmantels, and ceilings.

In neither of these houses, is the Federal style particularly apparent to the untrained eye—as is only natural since there is no sharp line of demarcation between the late Georgian and Federal, the differences being in the detail. Yet the difference is there, and in most instances, a distinctly Federal doorway is the key to the style. In adaptations of either style as encountered in different parts of the country, this distinction is often likely to be lost.

What these houses demonstrate, then, is that in spite of a monumental exterior in which dignity and restraint are emphasized, the Federal interior aimed at a less hidebound

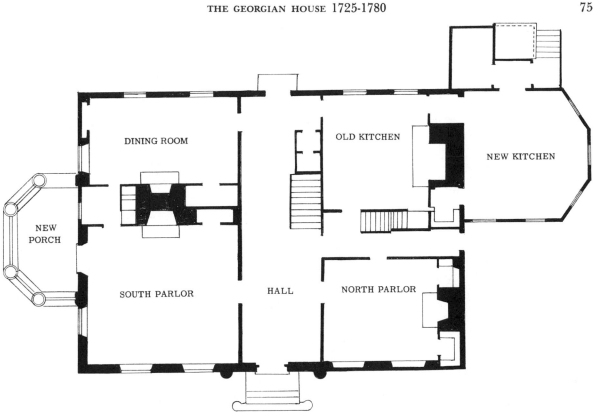

93. Floor plan of "The Lindens."

arrangement of rooms, and more functional space free from the restraint of rectangular areas. The curved walls, the alcoves, the elliptical rooms and rounded corners all contributed to free movement, a wider choice in furniture arrangement, and pleasanter and more interesting interiors. The need for something of the sort has been indicated in various attempts to break away from the rigid room arrangements of the Colonial styles. A notable example of this is seen in the Gardner-White-Pingree house in Salem, Massachusetts (Fig. 105). Such experiments also must have had their effect on the new classical style that was to dominate the American scene for the next forty years—that of the Greek Revival house.

94. Wister's Big House, "Grumblethorpe" in Germantown, Pennsylvania, is an interesting example of mid-18th-century Quaker-German architecture, with a Doric entrance.

1799

1806

1750

1744

1809

95. This series of elevations shows additions and changes to "Grumblethorpe" from 1744 to 1809—a unique record of the life history of an important house.

96. The Semple house (1780) may have been designed by Thomas Jefferson.

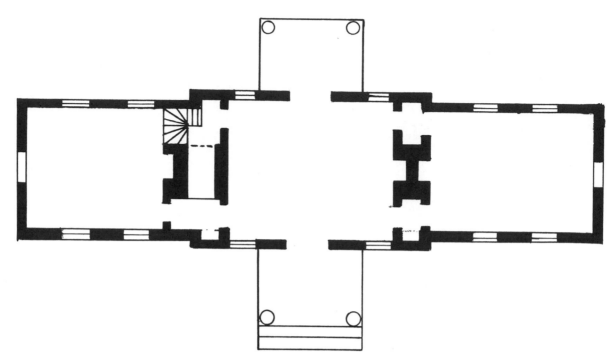

97. Floor plan of the Semple house.

98. The Judge Robert Pringle house in Charleston, South Carolina is Georgian with a Southern flavor—a typical single house with a beautiful door to the piazza, and a dormer on the roof hip.

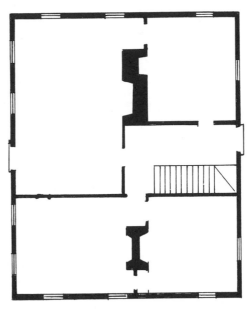

99. An early (1729) Charleston mansard-roofed double house of brick and stucco, with shed dormers, 2½ stories high plus street-level basement.

100. Plan of the Charleston "double house."

101. Cupola house at Edenton, N. C., shows certain New England features.

102. The Spencer-Woodbridge house in Savannah, Georgia illustrates the variety in detail of late eighteenth-century houses classified as Federal. This wooden house has the balanced façade demanded of this style, with classical porch and raised foundation. Otherwise it is entirely plain and, with the triple-arched chimney cap hidden behind the ridge, almost characterless.

103. This classic Pennsylvania stone house is said to have the handsomest exterior and interior woodwork in Chester County. The front is of dressed stone, the rest of rough fieldstone. The right-hand half of the house was built in 1806, the left-hand half added nine years later. This accounts for the middle dormer's being slightly off center. It will be noticed that the earlier windows have flat arches, the new ones none. There are two rooms on either side of a wide stair hall—altogether, a trim example of the Pennsylvania Federal style.

104. One of the first post-Revolutionary houses in Providence, R. I.: the John Brown residence, erected in 1786.

105. The Gardner-White-Pingree house, Salem, Massachusetts.

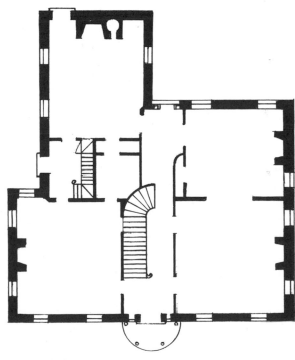

106. Floor plan of the house shows occasional rounded corners.

3

Greek Revival

The Greek Revival style has long been known as the architecture of the white pillars. In actuality, however, the external appearance of the Greek Revival house can range all the way from that of an austere Greek temple with windows (if such a thing can be imagined!) to that of a simple Colonial house with a massive square-posted porch over the front door. Though by definition the hallmark of Greek Revival architecture should have been pure Grecian classicism (in contrast with the Roman classicism of Georgian), with plain surfaces, dignity, and bold composition, in practice there is enough latitude between the two to permit the design and construction of a wide variety of charming and comfortable houses. That this goal was often achieved is seen in some of the examples given here, culled from among the thirteen original states—styles that set the pattern for many a house across the continent.

From about 1820 to 1840 the Greek Revival style overshadowed all competition. Beginning with the mansions and important public buildings of Washington, D.C., the style spread to those of adjacent areas, but was also copied in, or at least adapted to, numerous smaller dwellings from Maine to Virginia. In the next two decades it spread across the country; however, since we are here primarily concerned with the origins of, and the metamorphoses undergone by, architectural styles which were later to be adapted to new areas and new climates, we must first consider the Eastern beginnings of the style.

In New England, as elsewhere, the Greek Revival quickly became popular for public buildings in spite of the resurgence of Gothic and, in a lesser degree, of the Egyptian and the Italian villa styles. Greek Revival was in fact the first wholly American style, born along with the Republic; and its appeal was apparently universal. Soon it seemed that every city of consequence, and many another of little note, was anxious to become the Athens of America, even if in appearance only.

To take full advantage of the new style

107. Greek Revival with a Southern air in Massachusetts—a Provincetown house with fluted Doric columns stretched to 2-story height and equipped with dentilled echinuses to match the tiny dentils of pilasters, window and roof cornices. The delicate lyre-motif iron balustrade is reminiscent of New Orleans—Greek Revival at its prettiest and least monumental!

it was obviously necessary to develop a new house plan. This was done throughout the East and South, sometimes with unfortunate results. In this way regional types developed, ranging from virtual reproductions of the Temple of Athena to a cottage weighed down with a new portico and no visible sign of any other classical feature. In some instances the main entrance is in the principal façade; in others it occupies a gable end, or perhaps a recessed porch at one corner. There was no hard and fast rule.

The interiors of the better houses built in the Greek Revival style carried out the classic theme in the interior detail. Door frames were made wide, decorated with classical motifs, and crowned with a cornice. Twin pilasters separated the walls into panels, and

the anthemion was everywhere. Some of the modifications of Greek forms are creative, but many must be credited to ignorance. Both sorts will be observed in the regional photographs.

In this early part of the 19th century most of the Greek Revival buildings, large and small, were designed by architects—not by carpenters and builders. By its very nature, of course, Greek architecture was intended to be executed in stone. But in many regions wood was still the favored material, and a great many splendid wooden houses have been erected in this style.

The major characteristics of Greek Revival domestic architecture are those of the Greek temple—the use of pillared porticoes and pediments; the low or even flat roof, which was sometimes balustraded; and the suppression of chimneys. Doorways were all-important, and those houses which were without porticoes often were given heavy pilasters at the corners and flanking the doorways. And many an Old Colonial house was given a classic air by the addition of a Greek portico, or a massive porch and wide pilasters each end of the façade. Between 1820 and 1860 there were many variations on this theme, both regional and local, which form a fascinating study in themselves.

Greek Revival in the Central States and the South

The Greek Revival style proper originated in Washington, D.C., after the architect Latrobe had shown the way with his Bank of Pennsylvania at Philadelphia. Near-by areas were the first to adopt the new style. In Baltimore a number of large Greek Revival houses were built—in the 1830s and 1840s—which stand to this day. Some of these are more intimate and human than monumental. Both

108. Many a Greek Revival house began as a traditional dwelling with a classical porch added, as in this New England example.

109. This mansion, "Whitehall" in Maryland, is the earliest fully classical house surviving in this country, anticipating the Greek Revival temple form by thirty years. Originally low, with pedimented wings, it had a center entrance opening directly into a salon which occupied the full depth of the building, its coved ceiling at roof level. Built of brick with tall windows in the Virginia style having wide white frames with architraves, the central block could well withstand the raising of the wings to two full stories. The fluted Corinthian columns were hewn from single tree trunks. This mansion had the distinction of possessing the only interior water closet of Colonial times.

110. There is nothing essentially Greek Revival about this brick house in Alabama, with its end chimneys and central hall, except the huge wooden-pillared portico. The window trim is plain and the roof has no cornice or pediment. The decorative semicircular fanlight over the door, and the door itself, are framed in barely visible trim in weak contrast to the massive pillars and thick pilasters, suggesting a Southern Colonial type of house to which a Greek Revival porch has been added—a not uncommon practice in the 1830s and 1840s.

111. "Hampton," on the Santee River, South Carolina, is a Greek Revival plantation house that started life in 1735 as a small, 4-room, central-hall structure built by a Huguenot planter. Both ends were extended in 1758, one extension forming a 2-story ballroom, the other a high-ceilinged bedroom. To break up the large expanse of blank wall, window trim and blank shutters were added at the second-floor level. The pillared portico, which has some earmarks of the Federal style, was added in the late 1780s.

112. "Prospect Hill," Airlie, N. C.

113. This is the Belo house in Winston-Salem, North Carolina, a 2-story brick mansion of the late 1840s, with triple pediments facing the street supported by Corinthian columns which because of the exposed basement are three stories high. A similar portico on the garden side is two stories high. An important feature is the recessed front with its long cast-iron balcony, the central, unroofed portion passing through the porticoes. Miniature Corinthian columns support the outer sections of the balcony, with decorative cast-iron uprights and horizontal trim holding up the balcony wing roofs in the style of New Orleans.

individual and row houses have the same arched doorways, tall windows, and occasional columned porticoes. The larger houses often have their entrances at the side.

Richmond, Virginia also took up the style with enthusiasm, and an occasional Regency house showed the Greek influence in its murals. Elsewhere, in towns such as Alexandria, Norfolk, and Petersburg, the larger houses, aside from a few individual buildings, clung to the Georgian and Federal until late in the period. This pattern is representative of most of the Southern states, where conservatism seems to have combined with sudden, later flowering and strong local influences.

Farther west, in the Piedmont, settlers from Pennslyvania and Virginia swung the Greek Revival development into a different course. The Moravians and the Quakers contributed houses that were different in plan and exterior detail. Moravian buildings in Winston-Salem, though austerely simple, are beautiful with their hooded doors and brick-arched windows. Though the differences lessened with time, by the middle of the 19th century there still remained the contrast between the elegance and exuberance of the East and the quiet, formal dignity of what was then the West. For instance, "Prospect Hill" at Airlie, North Carolina (Fig. 112) has an early Republican air very like that of an 18th-century Connecticut house, with its classical porch, slender Doric columns and Adam trim—quite unlike anything else in this area. (Note chimney pent.)

In North Carolina, dampness and heat, combined with Virginia influences, led to Greek Revival houses with characteristic piazzas, having turned posts instead of classical columns to support a projection of the main roof. Two-story houses acquired a more classical appearance, giving towns like New Bern and Beaufort an air of elegance that had little to do with the size of the houses. The pattern was actually set, however, by the larger and more stylish dwellings.

In their two-story wooden houses, the Southerners had already achieved a certain classical distinction by the mere addition of pilastered and pedimented doorways and corniced windows. They knew the uses of paint and the architectural value of smooth, flat wood surfaces, which produced the effect of worked stone or stucco with little loss of textural warmth. Georgian was one thing, the cold correctness of Greek Revival another. And so Southerners needed time to think the new style over, to discover what they could adopt from it to give character and interest, and a "modern" feeling, to what they already had. No use rushing into something that might be just a passing—and somewhat extreme—fad. Elsewhere, of course, the growth of classical feeling—the gradual change-over from the Roman classicism of Georgian to the neo-classicism of Greek Revival—had been anticipated long before.

Greek Revival in New England

Few Greek Revival houses were built in New England before the middle of the 19th century. Occasionally a new house in the traditional manner would be given a Doric porch, but it was a long time before the idea of endowing the small house with a feeling of "classical monumentality" took hold. The early trend, rather, was to adapt a few Greek details to the familiar house just to keep up with the fashion, instead of merely copying Greek buildings whose style had little in common with the needs or outlook of the average man.

When the style finally did become popular, it apparently seemed that the simplest way of converting a Colonial house into a Greek temple was to turn the gable end to the street and incorporate the front entrance into it.

114. Another town house, the 2-story Small mansion in Macon, Georgia, combines square end pillars with Doric columns to support a classic entablature having a garland-decorated frieze. The flat and insignificant pediment is given interest by the anthemion decorations. The central balcony on heavy brackets adds to the total feeling of solidity, which makes it difficult to realize that this massive Greek Revival building is of wood, not stone.

By this means it was possible to make the gable into an impressive pediment, which would either remain flat or be extended to accommodate a row of supporting columns, thus forming a portico. This scheme of course introduced a revolutionary new floor plan, with an entrance hall along one side of the structure. This innovation in turn, necessitated a single file of rooms from front to back, in a manner anticipating the famous New York City "railroad flats." Occasionally there would be a gable-fronted house with a door at the side of the building, just to confuse matters. In most instances the interiors were given a Greek touch in the forms of the moldings and the fireplace mantels, while the single front room benefited by the taller and somewhat wider windows. Most of these houses were at least two stories high, the small single-story dwelling having extensions at the rear to accommodate additional rooms. These extensions were often narrower than the main body of the house by the width of the hall.

In other small Greek Revival houses, both pediment and portico were dispensed with. In their place the roof was made nearly flat and endowed with a high-coved cornice above the architrave to hide the peak. The effect was that of a flat-topped building, with the architrave and cornice and corner pilasters monumental in size. (See Fig. 119.) At the same time experiments were being made with other floor plans suited to the neo-classic style for the small house. However, before the demand for such houses in the lower price brackets could gain much momentum, the style had begun to be adopted for larger houses and mansions. In the beginning these seem to have taken their inspiration from the classical public buildings which were going up at a great rate in the expanding towns. The result was a number of imposing square houses with continuous colonnades, of which there are some splendid examples in places like Worcester, Massachusetts and Bangor, Maine. Many of these are somewhat heavy in design, angular and plainly monumental, with the Greek fret taking the place of the more frivolous anthemion or rosette favored by the then current books on Greek Revival design. The use of such frets became common, and they were even found as panel decorations on lintels, pilasters, and doors. A few years later that practice was largely abandoned. Elsewhere, differences in design are noted, due to the quality of the stone (the harder the material the simpler the decoration), to the climate, or simply to the habit of copying local quirks in design. In the colder areas the winter weather not only encouraged the retention of the Colonial idea of tacking on endless additions to the house, but favored the building of houses no more than a story and a half high. This permitted grouping the principal rooms on the main floor—a practice not limited to New England.

115. A Massachusetts Greek Revival house developed, thanks to an Ionic porch, from a traditional hip-roofed dwelling of 1789.

116. Even a little three-quarter house could be transformed by adding classical features such as a deep cornice and door architrave. The floor plan is incidental, as in this minimum example of Greek Revival.

Greek Revival Goes West

In spite of the fact that each architectural style is so different from the one it supersedes, nowhere does there seem to be a clean break between the one and the other. The transition may be rapid in certain areas but is usually gradual, and one of the most interesting aspects of this study of changing architectural fashions and their spread throughout the continent is the possibility of detecting relationships between the old and the new, and of ascribing specific features to certain cultural groups or areas. Almost always there

are prophetic indications of trends: in the classical touches given the traditional in anticipation of the Georgian; in the modified Georgian that led to the Federal; in the occasional house, found in both North and South, that suggested a temple long before the Greek Revival became the rage; and in the jigsaw brackets beneath classical cornices that heralded the coming of Victorian Gothic.

In tracing the spread of these styles, and of later ones, across the continent, a similar thread of continuity can be observed in very many instances. Others betray foreign influences—as, for example, in those where a

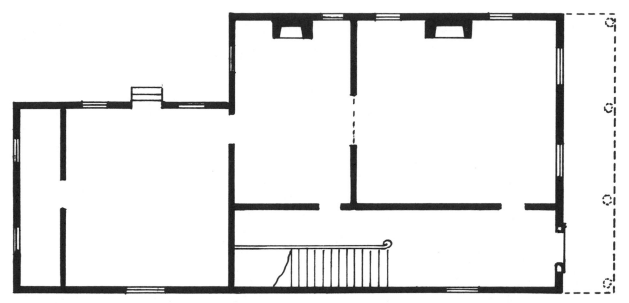

117. Floor plan of a basic New England Greek revival house.

118. In this gable-end-to-street example, the main entrance is at one side, so that the broad corner pilasters and architrave, set off by the bold caps, enframe six carefully spaced windows whose molded architraves lighten the effect, in spite of the modern diapered asphalt tiles that hide the texture of the siding beneath. The pedimented roof is lightened by returning the cornice only far enough to top off the entablature over the pilasters—minus a frieze, of course. Note that the upper windows are shorter than the lower ones, the latter having 6 over 9 lights, reversing the old-time order of early Colonial houses.

119. Even the foursquare, undecorated wooden Greek Revival house can form an attractive composition as this Connecticut house demonstrates: an effect heightened by the two-toned finish—white pillars and trim, with cornice, wall surfaces, and door a soft stone-brown. Built in the 1830s, it is severe in style but beautifully balanced, the façade neatly divided at transom level where the flush boarding ends and clapboard siding begins, the whole enframed in heavy corner pilasters surmounted by a solid-looking architrave and projecting cornice that hide a flattened roof. Channeling of the pilasters and porch pillars lightens the effect of solidity and creates interesting shadow lines. A projecting bay carries out the design, but interest is added by slightly arching its front-facing window and enclosing the whole in a molded architrave. No chimney is visible to spoil the composition.

builder has introduced characteristics of the houses of his homeland. Still other builders blended styles, or introduced modifications of the style native to their home colony or state. In investigating these influences, then, it is useful to follow the steps of the pioneers so that we may see and understand how American architectural history was made.

Shortly before the Revolution, settlers—mostly farmers, but including a few adventurers—were beginning to head through the Cumberland Gap from Virginia into the valleys of eastern Tennessee and spreading slowly northward into Kentucky. Thirty-five years later that trickle of settlement had become a flood, and the adventurers had been re-placed by men of substance—business men and financiers. Meanwhile settlers from Pennsylvania and Maryland, and even lower New England, took the westward trail through Pittsburgh and down the Ohio River, or followed the National Pike from Baltimore to Wheeling, West Virginia, and on to Zanesville. Most of the New Englanders, however, headed direct for "New Connecticut," the Western Reserve in Ohio. Crossing the Hudson, they made their way up the west side of the river into the Mohawk Valley, and thence along the shores of Lake Erie. Soon afterwards Greek Revival houses were being shipped in knocked-down condition to Tallmadge, Hudson, and a dozen other embryo towns. Meanwhile other settlers pressed on into Illinois and Michigan and Wisconsin. Thus the great westward trek began, culminating in the grand rush of 1849, which planted Eastern architecture on the West Coast.

In this way Ohio, Illinois, Indiana, Michigan, and Wisconsin were taken over by people from New England and northern New York State. Kentucky, Tennessee, and the southern areas were settled largely from the southern Atlantic seaboard. For this reason, in the states bordering Lake Erie we find houses in the New England style, and south of them many whose style originated in Virginia and

the Carolinas. And between their respective interpretations of the Greek Revival the main difference seems to center on the choice of whether to present the gable or the main façade to the front. In New England the gables seem to have been in the majority, at least for the medium-sized house; the builders of others compromised by planting a four-pillar portico in the middle of the main façade. In larger houses a square plan may have been adopted for the two-story central block, with its portico and pediment, plus one- or one-and-a-half-story wings—an arrangement particularly popular in New York State. There are a number of examples of this in

120. Even a brick Greek Revival house can have an air of trim neatness, as this New England house shows. Its windows are set in flush under fretted lintels, while the doorway is under a brick arch complete with keystone. The roof pediment and cornice, and the door with its surround, are the only deliberately decorative features. The entrance in particular adds a note of delicacy, with its two pairs of Ionic columns supporting an architrave that is decorated in low relief in the Adam manner, as are the thin cornice and the elliptical arch enclosing a sunburst fanlight—features more late Georgian than neo-classic, but none the less effective in this instance.

121. The Greek Revival style originated in Philadelphia and burst into bloom in Washington, where it is not surprising that builders
went overboard on it. Here is a gazebo, an
ornamental summer house, that was built in
Washington around 1825, complete with
twin pilasters, plain architraves, frieze and
cornice, and simple pediment; and surmounted by an octagonal cupola with a
domed top and arched windows. The tympanum is hardly more than a single board;
the rest of the building is of flush boarding.
At one time it must have formed the focal
point of a beautifully landscaped garden. It
shows in miniature the monumentality that
the early proponents of the neo-classical style
aimed for even in smaller houses.

is likely to be apparent.

It should not be surprising that for many settlers in the Midwest the New England Greek Revival was not entirely satisfactory. The Ohio farmers in particular seem to have preferred a modified T-shaped plan, with a recessed porch in the wing. (See Fig. 129.) This was thought to make possible a more flexible interior while allowing for the maximum of through ventilation. And, judging by the number built, it apparently worked. The origin of the floor plan, however, is not altogether clear. Similarly shaped Greek Revival houses with varying roof types and pilastered fronts (antae corners) are found in the Mohawk Valley. Others are recorded near Ashtabula, Ohio and Tipton, Michigan.

Be that as it may, between 1820 and 1860 many simplified Greek Revival houses were built throughout the Midwest, most of them less ornamented than their Eastern counterparts. The typical house had a roof of low pitch, inconspicuous chimneys, plain lintels and cornices, and painted walls. In Michigan, Ohio, and Illinois in particular, there were frame houses with good Greek doorways and window casings. After 1840, however, many of these houses acquired jigsaw brackets under the cornices. Ample porches came next; no Doric or Ionic pillars but thin, square posts, often with jigsaw ornaments. Finally, windows and doors acquired pediments and were otherwise ornamented. Victorian Gothic was obviously on the way.

It should be noted that in the South, even though the Spanish and French had divided Louisiana between them and put up some of their characteristic houses, neither style was copied or adapted to any significant degree. The French houses were for the most part half-timbered, the better ones being of stone. But with the Louisiana Purchase in 1803, the new arrivals preferred the Federal style, and later the Greek Revival. In the northwestern

Illinois and Michigan, whereas Ohio seems to prefer recessed porches and deep porticoes. In the South, and in particular on the plantations, two-story verandas helped provide the shade and coolness the climate demands, a feature that was to appeal to house owners from Texas to California. In very few instances, however, are any of the houses, Northern or Southern, copied in detail, and in the Southwestern states some Spanish influence

122. Not all westward-trending pioneers wanted the latest in building styles. Moravians in early 18th-century Pennsylvania used half-timber construction, and the builder of this 1850 house in Missouri—likewise a German—adopted the same idea with happy results. The brick-filled walls are plastered over and whitewashed on the outside, while the gables are clapboarded.

part of this area, however, Illinois still retained its French culture and sophistication. This fact may account, in part, for the handsome, wholly classical stone buildings that were put up there as early as the 1830 s.

While the Midwest was thus engaged in putting up its Greek Revival public buildings and private homes, the westward expansion continued. And the classic tradition survived the journey. In St. Louis tall houses were being erected with two-story porches like those of Tennessee, complete with roof deck and cupola. Arkansas and Iowa each put up a fine state capitol in Greek Revival style. The farmhouses of the Great Plains were like those of Ohio or the Eastern seaboard.

And so the tide rolled on into Oregon and Washington, where framed buildings with Greek Revival detail served for both homes and offices. In some instances the windows and doors were sent out by ship from New England. A little later these same ships were bringing complete structural units to a booming San Francisco.

In California gold-mining areas the fortyniners brought with them a taste for Greek Revival architecture and a number of knocked-down buildings as samples. The Greek Revival style therefore was flourishing —insofar as small houses are concerned—by 1850. A good example of the local style in wood is the Cady house at Sonora, almost in the center of the state, an early gold-mining area. This house has a pillared portico at one gable end, but the main entrance is in the center of the principal façade, sheltered by a pedimented porch. The end portico is carried around below the main roof level in the form of a shallow veranda, which joins the portico and continues on the other side of it to the far gable. The main door is flanked by flat pilasters supporting a heavy architrave with a flat cornice. Three transom lights span the door and its side lights. A curious combination of posts, pillars, pilasters, and columns, of stately portico and homely verandas, this house still unmistakably illustrates the Greek Revival influence on the frontier level.

In the following selection of Greek Revival

123. This beautiful 2-story, stucco-fronted brick house, dated 1850, is an excellent example of mansion-type Pennsylvania Greek Revival architecture at its best. The portico with its wooden, fluted Ionic columns and dentilled pediment seems, as indeed it is, an integral part of the gabled house which repeats the architrave, frieze, and cornice. A bracketed architrave of the same design ties the entrance door and its side lights together, balancing the three-section window above it. This flat-topped, three-section upper window has, incidentally, nothing in common with the Palladian. Inside, the house is well arranged, with the original kitchen in the basement. On one side of the central hall is a large drawing room with two fireplaces. On the other side are two rooms with a stairway between. Behind the main façade can be seen the later kitchen wing added in 1915, half concealed by the conservatory. On the other side is an added porch which was enclosed in the 1950 s.

houses erected in various parts of the Midwest and West will be observed the similarities and differences between them and their forerunners and contemporaries in the East. In each area some of the later houses will be seen to have acquired various touches that forecast the decline of Greek Revival and the burgeoning of the early Victorian—the classical giving way to the eclectic, the white columns to Gothic gingerbread.

In connection with these illustrations of Midwest Greek Revival houses which follow, it may be helpful to note certain fundamental influences on the design likely to be encountered in specific areas, *viz*:

Western Reserve populated from New England.

Chillicothe (as well as other parts of Southern Ohio) settled by Virginians.

French Canadians a strong influence in Detroit.

Cincinnati a river port and therefore a melting pot of races.

Cairo, Illinois, populated by French from New Orleans.

Many Germans in south and central Ohio.

124. The Baldwin-Buss house at Hudson, Ohio has an arched doorway and two french windows under the later porch—a Greek Revival type house that may very well have been shipped "knocked-down"!

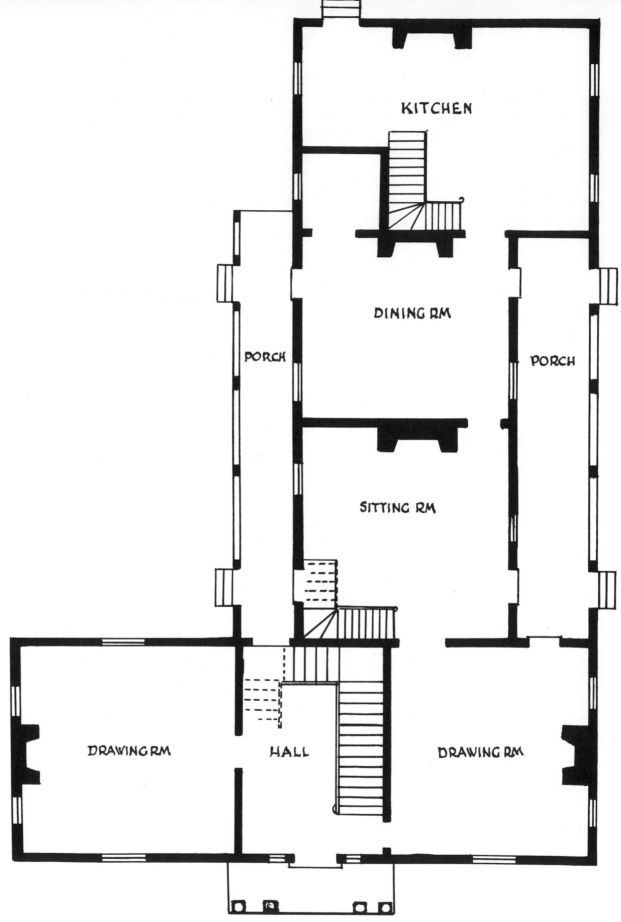

KITCHEN

DINING RM

PORCH

PORCH

SITTING RM

DRAWING RM

HALL

DRAWING RM

125. Floor plan of a Kentucky Greek Revival house.

126. In the Midwest not every pioneer was nostalgic for a Greek Revival house he had left behind. Captain Charles Ames, a veteran of the War of 1812, took with him memories of a New England farmhouse. In 1842, after living five years in a log cabin, he built himself this 1½-story, central-chimney, clapboarded house and wing at Pinola, Indiana, now restored to its former glory.

127. The Bentley house in Bentleyville, Ohio—a gable-end type Greek Revival house on the westward trail—with an unfortunate site that detracts from its impressiveness.

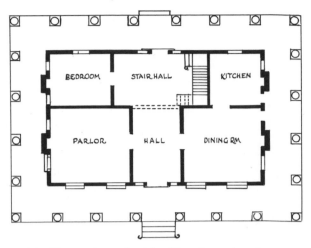

128. Floor plan of a Florida plantation house.

129. The Newton house, a Midwest farmhouse-type Greek Revival with recessed porch in wing.

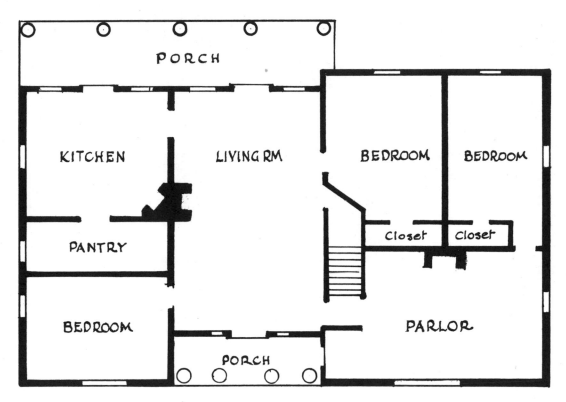

130. Floor plan of the Newton house.

131. Just over the northern Illinois border, at Lake Geneva, Wisconsin, another pioneer built himself a stone Greek Revival house, of the side-porch type, in 1851. The walls here are faced with cobblestones, relieved by dressed stone window and door sills and lintels, with quoins at all corners and openings except the windows. The pillars and pilasters of a recessed porch in the wing are flat and crude. The main entrance is in the end wall of the house. The cellar windows are spanned with flat arches of wedge-shaped, un-dressed stones that have the merit of not calling attention to themselves.

132. Built in 1785, could this be a forerunner of the Southern Greek Revival house? There are the pillars and the pilasters, the flattened pediment with large cornice molding, the flush-boarded typanum, an impressive double doorway with leaded transom and side lights, floor-length windows—all indicative of a well-designed classical façade far ahead of its time. This is "Anchuka," the Archer house at Port Gibson, Mississippi —an interesting survival.

133. A Greek Revival building in Oregon that has all the earmarks of Southern plantation architecture. Built in 1851, the Wolf Creek Tavern has since been much enlarged, as the plan indicates.

LADIES' PARLOR

BEDROOM

BEDROOM

PORCH

PORCH

HALL

DINING ROOM

KITCHEN

SHED

LOBBY

PORCH

134. Plan of the Wolf Creek Tavern.

135. A wooden, one-story Greek Revival, the Cady house, Sonora, California.

136 and 137. Although New England's saltboxes appeared in California in the 1830s, and the Greek Revival house ten years later, the adobe house long remained the favorite in the southern part of the state. The adobe walls were usually three feet thick at the base and two feet thick at the second-floor line, giving extra bedroom space. In the early houses the adobe was protected only by whitewash. Later it was covered with clapboards or vertical board-and-batten siding in the manner of Victorian "Steamboat Gothic." The low-pitched roofs were covered either with tiles or with hand-split shakes, and the ceilings finished in pine. The solid appearance of the adobe walls was relieved by the delicate porch posts and balustrades and shallow cornices front and rear, as these views of typical mid-19th-century ranch houses show.

138. The Jones House on State Highway 29 in southern Ohio was built by an early 19th-century pioneer who followed the Ohio River valley from Pittsburgh to the Scioto. Here he built this single-story house of dressed ashlar complete with square stone pillars and his own interpretation of Tuscan columns, plus a massive architrave and stone cornice. The end walls he carried up to form a low parapet for the metal-covered roof, terminating in a pair of stone chimneys. The house contains a center hall and four small rooms, and stands as square as the day it was built, as permanent a monument to Jasper Jones as he could have wished for, and a tribute to his original Pennsylvania home. One must admit, however, that it does have something of the air of a mausoleum.

Here are four Greek Revival houses built in Illinois in the mid-19th century: (Fig. 139) The Hoge house at Galena, brick, one-story, with a short portico fronting the main façade. Note the unimposing entrance as compared with that of Fig. 140, the Anson-Rogers house at Marengo. This is a full 1½-story portico type dwelling of wood, with center-spaced columns emphasizing the importance of the main doorway, whose side lights are enclosed by flanking pilasters and an architrave. An unusual feature is the applied parapet, set back from the eaves and paneled with lattice. The hipped - roof Dennison-Green house (Fig. 141) at Plainfield is square in plan, with central door, relying almost entirely on proportions and a balanced façade for its massive dignity. Fourth in this group is the mansion of the Mormon leader Joseph Smith at Nauvoo. (Fig. 143). Here, too, balance and proportion (aside from the single-hipped roof) are of considerable architectural merit; the rooms are high and the trim neat. Note the pilastered triple window over the entrance, unfortunately overemphasized by the dark paint.

139. The Hoge House, Galena, Ill.

140. The Anson-Rogers House, Marengo, Ill.

141. The Dennison-Green House, Plainfield, Ill.

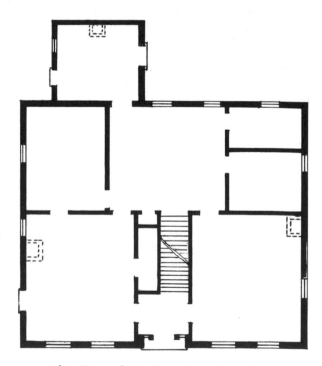

142. Plan of the Dennison-Green house.

143. The Joseph Smith House, Nauvoo, Ill.

In this group we have three Greek Revival specimens from Michigan. The Brooks house at Marshall (Fig. 144) is a brick mansion with five 2-story Ionic columns instead of the usual even number. This places one column in the center of the pedimented façade. The plainness of the pediment is more than counterbalanced by the large, ornate grouping of lights in its center, much in the manner of a door surround. The entrance to the house is located in a side porch, visible in the picture. In Fig. 145 we have a more modest but equally delightful single-story brick house of simple classical dignity. The four fluted Doric columns support a plain triangular pediment, the architrave, frieze, and cornice being carried along the sides of the building. The doorway here, set to one side under the portico in the New England manner, has both side lights and transom enclosed in an eared architrave, its visual "weight" nicely balancing the pair of floor-level windows. The portico floor and steps, being of stone, add an air of permanence. At Tecumseh is the one-story Anderson house (Fig. 146), which is a little earlier than the other two and, though of wood, somewhat more monumental because of the heavy roof balustrade and cupola. The first floor, with its graceful fluted Doric columns and simple architrave, plus the balanced wings which carry out the feeling, is altogether excellent. The superstructures detract from this by introducing a cluttered effect, which the balustrade spindles do nothing to diminish. The house does, however, indicate the high aspirations of the Michigan pioneers.

144. The Brooks House, Marshall, Mich.

145. The Wright-Brooks House, Marshall, Mich.

146. The Anderson House, Tecumseh, Mich.

147. In 1836 Sylvanus Wade, a young blacksmith, headed west from his home in North Adams, Massachusetts, to build the first house in a place he named Greenbush, in wild Wisconsin territory. While living in a log cabin with his wife and nine children he built the latest thing in village-style Greek Revival houses—this 1½-story, hip-roofed dwelling with deep eaves and cupola. The recessed porch has five doors giving access to the entrance hall and to three individual rooms. Upstairs, what appear to be eyebrow windows of the "lie-on-your-stomach" sort actually are about three feet from the floor, and designed so as not to spoil the line of the architrave.

148. Seven years later, in 1851, stagecoach service having been established, Wade built this inn along the lines of the original house but 2½ stories high, with a ballroom on the top floor. It will be noticed that the roof of the 2-story portico is well below the top-floor windows and so does not interfere with the effect of the main cornice with its nicely shaped openings and deep frieze. Both house and inn are, in fact, handsome in a substantial way, and there is no mistaking their style.

149. When the Mormons moved from Illinois to Utah they took with them ideas for Greek Revival architecture. Here is one of their largest and most famous houses, "The Beehive," which Brigham Young built (and populated)—a 2-story ashlar and stucco structure with a cupola. This is a Greek Revival mansion of about 1855, which the tall pillars and veranda invest with a Southern air.

150. In certain areas of Texas the smaller wooden Greek Revival house was quite abreast of the times in 1850, as this view of the Collins house near Crockett shows. Neat and unobtrusive, it has both scale and charm, as well as individuality.

4

Houses of the Victorian Era

The term Victorian as applied to American domestic architecture covers a wide variety of related styles developed during the Victorian era—1836 to 1900. Although based largely on the medieval Gothic style, the Victorian Gothic soon became adulterated with Italian, French, Tudor, and Oriental details. One of its chief merits was that it gave the architect a great deal of freedom in developing a floor plan to meet a variety of individual needs. Where the Greek Revival interior plan was governed by the foursquare exterior and the formal door and window placement, the Victorian Gothic was planned from the inside out. It could be added to in any direction, and usually was. Wings, bays, projections of any kind could be stuck on at any angle, and the whole to some degree unified by the exterior decoration, or held together by an all-embracing veranda. Actually, this style permitted of more comfort and convenience than the more classical designs, with possibilities for natural expansion of the building.

Transitional Traditional

By 1840 a great many small houses in the 18th-century traditional style had been built as unpretentious, utilitarian homes; the early ones with a braced frame, the later ones with the new balloon frame, although they were externally similar. These simple dwellings were two stories high, either with a central chimney or with one at each end. Now that stoves were available, chimneys were smaller and fireplaces fewer. Windows were larger, with fewer panes, and the trim severe. This was the basic style of the period, and with the coming of the Victorian styles soon acquired transitional characteristics.

Here, for example, is a simple two-story wooden house in the traditional style, with a central chimney designed for stoves. The eaves and gable are moderately deep, placing its construction fairly late in the 19th century. Victorian additions include a square, pedimented bay centered at second-floor level.

151. Sharply pitched roofs and decorative bargeboards were basic features of the small Victorian cottages advertised widely in mid-century. Here is one such cottage, together with the simple plan of a somewhat larger example of the so-called rural retreat.

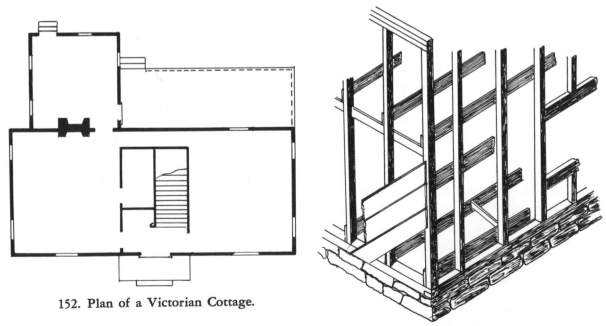

152. Plan of a Victorian Cottage.

153. Detail of a balloon-frame construction.

This is a well-proportioned structure, reminiscent of a Georgian pavilion. Below it, the entrance hall is extended two or three feet farther outward to the front door, which has side lights extending down to floor level. Over the door is still another extension, this time with a pedimented roof, forming a shallow, open porch. It is this porch, with its turned posts and spindles, that supplies the Victorian air, a feeling emphasized by parallel enclosed porches that extend the full length of the house. In this example, as in some others analyzed here, the Victorian additions by no means cheapen the structure. There is nothing flimsy about the additions or the multiplicity of turnings. As will be noted from the picture, the large windows of the front rooms are inside this framing of posts, arched brackets, and spindled panels. Even the tinted glass

—so beloved of the later Victorians—seen in the upper sash of the "pavilion" is more intriguing than offensive to our modern eye.

Fig. 155 is another simple traditional house, but this time of stone, with an interesting history of transitional remodeling. It was built in 1841, with narrow end chimneys designed for use with stoves, and an almost flat roof. When it was remodeled in the 1880's, the first Victorian addition evidently was the large cross-gable with its double dormer window. The upper half of this gable, which in shape is far from that of a classical pediment, is decorated with shingles arranged in a semicircular pattern and now painted dark green, while the lower half, containing the pair of windows, is faced with white clapboards. The second addition is a deep porch, returned at both ends. Its pillars are carried on square-

154. A 2-story traditional house with Victorian additions.

155. A traditional end-chimney stone house remodeled with Victorian porch and cross-gable.

156. A mid-19th century cottage with Victorian decorations that really add charm.

paneled bases. Surmounting them is a deep frieze with closely spaced brackets under the eaves. Each of the posts flanking the entrance has a pair of brackets, and topping that section of the frieze is a low pediment, its tympanum painted dark green with a white half-moon ornament at its bottom center.

The white mortar outlining the dark random-ashlar blocks creates an interesting pattern in both shape and color, with which the long frieze, broken up by the succession of brackets, tones in happily. Only the cross-gable itself is overpowering, because of its size and surface textures, which give it the appearance of an afterthought hastily tacked on. In spite of this, the house is an attractive example of transitional design with a distinctive character of its own.

This third and last example of transformations to invest an earlier traditional house with a Victorian air is, though appealing, a minor one. (See Fig. 156.) Fashion affects most of us more than we may realize. In this charming single-story cottage we can detect the same human urge to break away from tradition, to keep abreast of the times. The simplest answer to the problem here (since the porch was evidently original) would have been to introduce a gay note of gimcrackery. Whose obscure genius it was that solved the problem with a bandsaw by cutting out those fanciful silhouettes and letting them into the tops of the porch posts, we shall never know. But the fascinating result is there for all to see.

At this same time Goth and Greek were locked in a battle for survival. Many a handsome Greek Revival house succumbed to the popular urge to be in fashion, and by 1850 the Greek style was definitely passé. Some instances of this Victorian cannibalism are here pictured and briefly described:

In this first example, behind a fancy façade we can still distinguish an imposing stone Greek Revival house with dentilled cornices. Though there appears to be three stories, this is in reality a two-story house built into a steep bank so that the basement is above ground at street level. A little over a hundred years ago, the owner tried to achieve the best of both worlds in blending the neoclassical and Victorian styles. The porch and veranda with their long rows of turned balusters, gleaming white against the gray stone, might well have destroyed what character the building had. Here, however, the balustrades have been absorbed into a two-story structure composed of nicely proportioned pillars topped by a richly carved pediment. The whole is flanked by eaves cornices, with dentils that match those of the main building. Old and new are thus neatly tied together, so far as wood and stone structures can be blended, the roof pediment and cornices serving as the connecting links. (See Fig. 157.)

Another example shows how thoroughly a Greek Revival house can be submerged beneath Victorian additions. We can still see the roof pediment and the mutilated architrave, frieze, and cornice on parts of two sides. There are also a pair of floor-length windows, no longer shadowed by a portico. Instead there is a mid-century two-story bay window, with a somewhat skimpy bracketed cornice at upper and lower ceiling levels. Over the front door is a pillared porch, its hipped roof surmounted by a three-sided bay front. The gable roof above this has its architrave and frieze cut off at an angle to match the line of the window below. Filling in that angle is a pair of fancy brackets with a turned drop at their junction. This house shows clearly some of the difficulties of reconciling two very different styles. (See Fig. 158.)

Something of an enigma is this small house (Fig. 159) which looks as though it may originally have been something else. Perhaps it once had a steeper roof, or maybe a Greek

157. A more or less successful attempt to combine neo-classic with Victorian style.

158. This house shows how thoroughly Greek Revival can be submerged by Victorian additions.

Revival pediment—a suspicion based on the wide corner boards and those tall front windows. In any event, the Victorian urge has caught up with it, and today its eaves are adorned with a delicate and engagingly pretty example of jigsaw scrollwork. Equally fragile in appearance are the porch posts, like clustered flower stems, arching out toward the top into brackets almost round in section.

Victorian Eclecticism

Most of the foregoing transitional houses were converted long after the Victorian designs they were intended to imitate had become the vogue throughout the country. Of the true exemplars of the Victorian, those illustrated next are among the less extreme in design and decoration.

Since the 1830 s publishers had been turning out booklets of cottage designs to take advantage of the new constructional methods afforded by the availability of dimension lumber in small stock sizes. By the 1850's they had covered the whole gamut of Victorian styles with these romantic edifices—Rural Castellated, Bracketed Gothic, Pointed or Tudor, Old English, Italian Villa, Elizabethan, Rustic Pointed, and even a flat-roofed "Tuscan," so-called, dripping a myriad wooden icicles.

In the larger and more substantial houses there was an equal enthusiasm for the new styles and the new way of building. Together they permitted greater latitude as to plan and simplified the adding or subtracting of space without detracting from the over-all appearance. Every known building feature was called into play during the next fifty years—but-

159. Steamboat Gothic additions to a nondescript.

160. Not every house with its second story hidden behind a mansard roof is so successful in design and appearance as this one. A roof of this sort is heavy and imposing in appearance, and usually calls for a taller building. There is, however, no lack of proportion here: the dormers break up the solid surface, and the delicate cresting adds a touch of lightness. This feeling is repeated in the treatment of porch posts and decorative spindles. The wide spacing of the posts and the sweeping curve of one porch end give an open, spacious effect, a lightness and airiness, while the turned drops centered between the posts break the monotony of the spindle band. Here, too, the plain pedimented dormers tone in nicely with the bay window below. Even the jigsaw brackets of the rear porch posts are in keeping with both period and design.

tresses, medieval window moldings, clustered chimney stacks, five-sided bay windows, cathedral carving on stair newels, latticed lights, balusters, porches, columns, cottage windows, colored transoms Romanesque round arches, shingled walls, broad roofs, wide piazzas—all regardless of origin or suitability. Nevertheless, in spite of this orgy of styles promoted largely by enthusiastic carpenters who saw no further need for architects, some excellent homes were built, and proved not only roomy and convenient, but also light and airy, before being crammed to the point of suffocation with late-Victorian furniture and furnishings.

Thanks to the flood of literature on the subject, and to ready-made designs that any carpenter could copy, houses similar in overall appearance and plan came to be built independently in various settled sections of the United States. However, so much leeway was allowed the builder in dressing up a house that there was no need for any two to look alike. And with the same basic styles available everywhere there was little point in going far afield for inspiration. The same basic sort of house was being built everywhere, and regional differences were practically non-existent.

Externally, the early American Gothic houses were comparatively simple in design, their decorative details having been intended originally to be executed in stone. Stone carving was expensive, however, and thus necessarily limited to mansions. For most people such decorations had therefore to be limited to such as could be rapidly and cheaply sawn out of wood. The availability of cheap applied decorations encouraged builders to throw away their books on Gothic architecture and rely on what was termed "gingerbread" instead of good basic design. Such houses are now referred to as "Carpenters' Gothic."

The Rise of American Gothic

In spite of an increasing tendency toward

161. Here is a contemporary house with the central gabled porch extended into a forward wing. This wing is tied to the main body of the house by a full width porch. At first glance it is not evident that this is a T-shaped house at all. In a comparison of the two houses it will be seen that this one still retains the brackets supporting the gable roof—but in place of the crossed timbers is a decorative triangular panel whose pierced design has a fretwork apron underneath. Almost hidden behind this apron is a tiny pent roof, similarly decorated, which acts as a canopy over tall twin windows. These windows extend upward into the gable, where the same vertical boarding is used. Four dormers on this level, breaking through the eaves overhang, have triangular roofs which extend well forward and are decorated in a similar manner. The porch probably is the feature that dominates the rest, with its square-ended turned posts and jigsaw brackets. The two central posts are omitted, their places being taken by pendant stumps with inverted pyramidal ends. The porch rail is much simpler, the angles of the x-members being filled with cut-out inserts of a design subdued enough not to detract from the scrollwork above.

162. A distinct departure from any of the above is this Roman Gothic or Italianate house. Because of the way the ell portion is attached to the arcaded façade, a number of questions need to be asked about this building. It would seem that the substantial square-pillared portico was original and may at one time have extended the full width of the house. With its Roman arches and Gothic windows, together with the steep roof and equally precipitous cross-gable containing another pointed window, it would form a true Gothic Revival house. If the ell portion had been turned in line with it, the house would have been about twice as long, with a pair of cross-gables to break up the roof expanse.

As the picture shows, with the present arrangement the two cross-gables look into one another's windows—an unpleasant case of strabismus. This is, however, merely a more than usually obvious indication of what has, or may have, happened to so many of these old houses; few of them today are as they were sixty to eighty years ago, and it is quite certain that many built in a Victorian style have been changed in one way or another over the years. These things therefore need to be considered in determining the original style.

florid and often meaningless decoration, the style had the advantage of a flexible plan. It could be added to in almost any direction. Its fault lay largely in the exterior extravagances indulged in by the carpenter-designers. "Carpenters' Gothic" went in for steep gables, where no gables were needed or where dormers would have served just as well; pointed windows, combined with vertical board-and-batten siding to accentuate the height; towers were capped with peaked roofs; the houses with hexagonal or pilastered chimneys. Hipped roofs were dressed up with cross-gables; windows with diamond panes; loggia roofs were supported by flat pillars pierced with decorative designs. Square-topped windows were spanned by Tudor-style dripstones. Gothic mansions sported Tudor-style decorative bargeboards and Elizabethan clustered chimneys. By the time of the Civil War such mansions had acquired bay windows, and most ground-floor rooms opened onto terraces and loggias through french windows made necessary by the deep and gloomy porches.

One of the early Victorian styles was the

Italianate. This was at once Americanized by reproducing it in wood. The balloon frame and clapboard siding had to accommodate Gothic arches, round-headed windows, and scrollwork, with fancy brackets holding up the deep and heavy cornices. As time went on the cornices became more elaborate and heavy, the brackets larger and more fanciful. In the East this led to renaming the style as "Hudson River Bracketed." By 1845 the earmarks of the Italianate style were a tall, square tower with round-topped twin windows, pseudo-clock faces harboring trefoil lights, a balcony with a scalloped hood, and occasionally a square-pillared porch and a flat-topped, octagonal, one-story wing. Some towers had twin trefoil or quatrefoil windows, and balconies on all four sides. Another echo of the Italian villa would be cubical in form,

with a large octagonal cupola on the flat roof. Other features of this style were deeply molded eaves, heavy brackets, and tall windows.

Following the end of the war, decorative extravagances reached new heights. Houses were built with parapets, turrets, crocket-ornamented pinnacles, and oriel windows. This was the General Grant period—an unfair appellation since that great general neither started the fashion nor followed it. In this period, much wooden gingerbread gave way to cast iron; it was the era of quoins and colored glass, and of trim painted in violently contrasting colors. This was the day also of the mansard roof—a fashion that lasted until about 1876. All houses of two stories or more (and many of a single story) were crowned with this "French roof," steep-sided and flat-

163. The cubical Victorian house with a cupola is found in many states, but this Italianate specimen from Alabama would be hard to beat for style, so well does it lend itself to the dignity of the 2-story pillars and Roman arches—a theme repeated in the cupola windows. Both impressive and decorative is the cast-iron balcony beneath the portico, an innovation introduced in the 1840s by iron-founders in the North.

164. A later Victorian house that seems to be pretty much in its original condition is this "wedding-cake" design. All-white, including the roof, it has a dignity which is not impaired even by the extravagantly decorated chimney with its curlicues and brackets and its paneled base. Here is the familiar cross-gable, richly ornamented with a carving resembling a clock face. Beneath the gable is a triple window with pilasters and a gracefully arched cornice. The porch pillars are substantial and square, with bases and capitals and, of course, brackets. But it is the porch pediment, broken to receive a crown-shaped ornament, that adds the finishing decorative touch to this Victorian dream-house of the 1870s.

topped, which went around the four sides of a house and accommodated no less than two ornate dormers to a side. Most of the roofs were crowned by a fancy wrought- or cast-iron cresting.

In the 1880 s the trend switched toward the Oriental—minarets and horseshoe arches, Egyptian pylon gateways, and temple fronts with inward-leaning (battered) walls, plus a nod toward Byzantium in the onion-domed towers. For smaller houses, however, the simple Gothic style hung on, albeit drowned in a sea of wooden lace.

Following are some examples of each style, most of which have the merits of high ceilings and roominess, and of having been convertible into comfortable homes for today.

For the next thirty years these styles were copied, with variations, gradually becoming modified as the architect showed the way to

careful design in place of unrestrained decoration, utilizing color and texture with a
growing tendency to return to classic forms.
And so the more sober Victorian passed into
history with the dawn of the 20th century.

Now we are finding that many houses of this
period can be transformed into comfortable
homes which it would be prohibitively costly
to duplicate today.

165. A somewhat later and more rigidly formal Victorian small house having not only a pair of
steep cross-gables but a gabled pavilion as well. The tiny pierced decorations of the bargeboard, door hood, and hood brackets are so small as to be barely noticeable. Even the window
architraves have a minimum of molding its function being to deflect rainwater rather than
to give character to the façade. The one exception to the general restraint is the pointed, center window with its deep drip molding. The total effect is that of a very plain, very tall
wooden house with an immense roof, upon the apex of which perch a couple of spindly
chimneys. Undoubtedly this was someone's protest against the overdressed houses of the 1880s.

166. In sharp contrast with the foregoing façade is this very similar house, built about ten years later. Its most noticeable feature is the profusion of heavy timber cross-braces and brackets. In place of a pavilion is an enclosed balcony over an open porch. Above the balcony is a cross-gable no more than half the height of the roof. At the rear is a taller gable, which intersects the main roof slightly below the peak. All four gables have deep overhangs held up by crossing timbers and heavy triangular brackets. The siding in these gables consists of vertical boards with narrow strips covering the joints. Clapboards are used below, providing the much-needed horizontal accent. Under the pavilion gable is a band of applied fretwork, the only other conscious decoration being the porch rails and newel posts. Windows are rectangular, tall, and plain. Many farmhouses of this sort were erected during the last quarter of the 19th century.

167. This massive mansion is of somewhat later date than the foregoing—probably around 1880, during the period of the American Renaissance. Here we have the typical elaborate turned posts and the scalloped shingles surmounted by the pebble-dash panels of a pseudo-half-timbered gable. The deep, decorated bargeboards and the open third-floor balcony, overtopped by a massive square chimney with a cluster of "pots," all serve to underline the impression of solidity and substantial construction, and add to the feeling of sturdy compactness. Here, too, we have a comparison between the two rounded porches, with the same sweeping row of delicate spindles. In this case, however, the spindles are bulbous and carried between a heavy lower framing member and the porch eaves that expose the rounded rafter ends. The connecting brackets between the twin posts suggest miniature Moorish arches, adding a further exotic note to a late-Victorian mansion that is far from monotonous from any aspect.

168. Proof that it does not take stone tracery to give a stone house a Victorian air is evident in this figure. Here is a 2½-story Pennsylvania mansion of blue marble and limestone built in 1865, whose decorative details are almost all in wood. Its massive bracketed style combines some architectural features of the German *schloss,* the French cottage, and the Swiss villa. The foursquare tower has heavy stone balconies and round-headed triple windows, topped off by a roof with four gables centered around what seems to be a vestigial mansard. The entrance porch has heavy wooden pillars in groups of three, with arching brackets, reflecting the massive solidity of the building itself. In spite of its imposing external appearance, this house is remarkably comfortable and well-arranged, with a wide through hall, a service wing, and a fireplace in each room—one reason why it is still occupied by descendants of its builder.

169. Here we have a somewhat austere example of the late bracketed mansion, with only a vestigial mansard innocent of dormers. The principal windows have Tudor-style "drip-stones"—of wood, naturally—while the third floor and dormers are arched in the Roman style. Applied decoration is confined to the fancy eaves brackets with their terminal drops, and the sculptured porch posts, solid and square, which scarcely need the pendant drops suspended from their cornice. The heavy, rounded arches of the porch give it a welcome solidity and an air of permanence, with the result that the porch itself is one of the very few shown here that look like a part of the building they adorn.

170. This is a more spectacular mélange, consisting of an octagonal mansard roof with an elaborate cresting, on a three-story tower, and a hint of Tuscan in the flat-arched roof of the cupola. Most of the windows are in the round-topped Roman style, with heavy moldings and blinds to fit. The porch is rather delicate for such a solid house, with curved brackets to match the window-top moldings. Aside from the tower with its paneled frieze, decorated parapet, fish-scale slates, fancy dormers, and intricate iron cresting, the architecture is remarkably restrained and clean-cut. The period, we should say, is probably around 1860–1865.

171. Another large wooden house of this same period combines a number of architectural influences. Here is the imposing square tower of the Italian palazzo, crowned with a sweeping mansard roof that terminates in a railed lookout. This rather squat roof incorporates twin, flat-topped dormers, heavily framed and corniced in keeping with the general solidity of the structure. Inside the large pediment of the main gable is a triple window reminiscent of Georgian Palladian, while twin, round-topped windows on the tower side acknowledge Roman origins. On the ground floor, a metal roof over the square bay introduces an Oriental note. A variation in surface textures is obtained by the use of fancy shingles at base and roof levels, on the upper section of the tower, and on the rear extension.

The later period to which this style belongs is indicated by the added ornamentation on window architraves and porch brackets. Altogether it is an interesting example of the successful combination of ideas from various sources. And, like so many of its kind, this house is well built, commodious, and convenient.

172. In the mid-19th century a great many Victorian frame houses with flat roofs and recessed entrance porches were built in New England. This house suggests, in its foursquare shape and clean lines, a somewhat less than rigidly classical Greek Revival residence. The Victorian touch here lies in the crown of wooden "icicles" that encircles the roof both of the house proper and of its annex. A Greek Revival touch is seen in the heavy, plain lintels, and in the eared architrave of the entrance door. This house is painted a pale yellow with white trim, and is even more resplendent in the winter sun than appears in the picture.

173. A well-known example of design run riot is the Wedding Cake house in Maine. Originally a staid brick house built in 1826, it was imbedded in wooden Gothic decoration in 1850. Note the Palladian window inside the decorated Gothic arch!

174. The Van Buren house at Kinderhook, New York is an unhappy example of old Colonial architecture defaced with pretentious Victorian gimcrackery. This 18th-century, 2-story brick house was altered in the 1850 s, the lovely Palladian window, the stair dormers, and the classic porch mutilated beyond recognition while an added Italianate tower with Moorish arches accents the absurdity.

175. Among the happier results of Victorian eclecticism is the T. Macdonough Russell house at Middletown, Connecticut, a pure example of Victorian Gothic that is just as attractive today as when it was built in the mid-19th century.

176. A fine example of the medieval Gothic, plus a battlemented tower that has nothing in common with either the lancet windows or the heavy cast-iron finials from the owner's foundry. This was built between 1842 and 1852 at Lexington, Kentucky.

177. Built in the 'fifties in old-time Salem, Massachusetts, this Gothic Revival house with its twin gables and its pyramidal finials and fence posts, must have struck an ultra-modern note. Note that the fence pattern is repeated in the balcony balustrade.

178. Even in the Missouri of the 1850 s, carpenters were seeking the unusual in Victorian Gothic, as witness this example from the vicinity of Peveley, with its steep gables, ornate finials, and pointed windows. Stripped of these non-essentials it would no doubt make a home eminently satisfactory to the modern taste.

179. Here is a fine example, in masonry, of the ultra-dignified Italianate Victorian mansion from Portland, Maine—the work of a competent architect and a refreshing contrast to similar houses attempted in wood.

180. The record would not be complete without one example of "Moorish Revival"—this from Natchez, Mississippi, fittingly known as "Nutt's Folly," begun in 1860 but never finished.

181. Very much like a house in appearance is this late-Victorian inn, the Trocadero at San Francisco, California. It is an excellent example of the Eastlake style dating from 1870. Note the cast-iron cresting, the massive cross-gable sheltering the entrance pediment, the colored glass and the four-gabled cupola—an interesting note on which to conclude our survey of two hundred years of American houses.

5

An Architectural Melting Pot

The main distinguishing features of many old American houses vary not only geographically and chronologically but also according to the national or cultural background of the builder-owner. Thus, although the locality settled by any one group may be a good guide to the style of architecture to expect, it is possible that compromises may have been made in any one structure. This is particularly true of the eastern colonies in the late 17th and early 18th centuries, when the first massive invasion from Europe was at its height. Immigrants poured in through the port of Philadelphia, and most of them immediately went on to what appeared to be greener fields—north to New Jersey, east to Delaware and Maryland, and southwest down the Virginia Valley.

This actually marked the beginning of the westward trend, which, however, was balked both by the French on the Mississippi and by the hostile Indians. The migrants thus perforce turned south toward the Carolinas and Georgia. It was these circumstances, then, that finally brought about a great blending of architectural styles over an area extending from the Hudson to the Susquehanna, from Bethlehem to Savannah, and down the Great Valley itself.

Though they may originally have established their own settlements, most of these individuals and groups eventually came to influence one another in various ways, including building methods, house design, and architectural features. If we are to understand the local variations in house design, we need to have some idea of the racial and ideological composition of the groups responsible for them.

To state the matter briefly, then, by 1700 trails had been opened both between the North and the South, and between the Tidewater and the mountains, and here is what happened:

Germans coming in through Philadelphia spread over Pennsylvania and up the Lehigh Valley to the Delaware Water Gap. Swedes claimed the upper end of Delaware Bay to the Water Gap, but Jersey Quakers moved in on them.

141

Lutheran Salzburgers settled on the Savannah River.

Scots settled on the Alamaha.

Scotch-Irish groups from the Maryland border drifted west and south, on the way settling the western slopes of the Valley of Virginia, while German-speaking groups occupied the eastern slopes.

Huguenots from Virginia founded Bath, North Carolina, while other Huguenots, Germans, and Swiss built New Bern.

Albemarle Point was taken over largely by English colonists from Barbados.

Charleston, South Carolina, was the biggest melting pot of all, having been settled by small groups of Irish, Welsh, Scots, Dutch, and migrant New Englanders, the dominant groups being English, French Huguenots, and Barbados planters.

From South Carolina, Moravians moved on to land granted to them in North Carolina in the vicinity of Bethlehem, Salem, and Bethania. And it was the German-speaking Moravians, the Swiss, and the Scotch who moved into Georgia.

These various cultural groups, each with its own building traditions, naturally influenced one another as they populated the middle and lower coastal states. For example, the so-called Quaker house plan was soon to be found all the way from New Jersey to South Carolina. Today it would be quite difficult to determine precisely what was contributed by each national group to the various architectural styles developed over this extensive area. However, the following tabular list of regional characteristics may serve as a guide to probabilities where no other clue exists.

External Earmarks of New England Colonial

Early: Plain, foursquare, center-chimney type, of wood.

182. Thin sash, wide muntins, with wavy glass set flush, are earmarks of early date.

183. Outdoor bake ovens and smoke houses were common in late 18th-century Pennsylvania. This one, combined with a well, is near Gettysburg.

Roof: ridge or gambrel.

Door and window trim: plain.

Door: vertical boards, or simple paneled.

Plain transom, four or five lights.

Windows: heavy muntins, small panes, set flush; 9/6, 12/8, or 12/12.

Siding: clapboards or shakes.

Roof: shingled, eaves flush, no gable overhang.

Foundation: floor level.

Overhang (if any): hewn, single or double (at second floor and gable levels).

Chimney: large, centered.

Stories: one, one-and-a-half, two, two-and-a-half.

Types: Cape Cod, saltbox, early American one-room-deep, two-rooms-deep, half-, and three-quarter houses.

Variations: masonry-ended houses, with chimney in one or both end walls; single-story with sprung eaves or pedimented porch; Rhode Island stone-ender, one stone gable wall with chimney.

Late: Doors: (1) pilasters, architrave, frieze, cornice (also transom); (2) triangular or segmental pediment; (3) broken pediment triangular or swan's-neck). Double (two-leaf) doors may have transom, with rectangular or tombstone lights.

Moldings: may be of classic form, but members not classic in composition or contour. (This distinguishes them from the formal early Georgian.)

Chimneys: traditional center-hall, late Colonial houses may have two chimneys on ridge or in gable walls.

External Earmarks of Northern Colonial

184. New England 17th-century bake ovens were located at the back of the fireplace. In the 18th century they were moved to the side.

Dutch:

Two or more chimneys.

High, ridge roof, two rooms deep (granary in peak).

Stone walls, wooden gable above tie beam.

Flush eaves and gables.

Brick walls, steep parapeted roof; gable incorporates end chimneys.

Bake ovens protrude from end walls.

Flat arches over wood lintels.

Dutch cross-bond brickwork, patterned or plain.

Cantilevered door heads, dished upper side (pediment type dished underside).

Solid shutters.

Double transoms.

Shed dormers.

Dutch doors, bull's-eye lights in panels, tomb-

185. Early Pennsylvania German fireplaces often have the cheeks hollowed out where they meet the face, as this picture shows.

stone lights.

Built-in bed-places.

Decorative iron beam anchors.

Flemish:

Wood houses, two rooms deep, end chimneys, "Dutch" gambrel roof.

Flush gable, flared eaves ("Dutch kick").

Flared eaves extended to form porch roof (with or without pillars).

Stoep with seats.

Wide clapboards—long wall shingles without corner boards.

Stone houses, stone ends one foot above eaves; shingled above.

Flemish bond brickwork.

External Earmarks of Southern Colonial

186. Early Hudson River Dutch houses often had double transoms above the Dutch doors.

Maryland:
Chimney pents.
Distinctive gambrel.
Jerkin-head roof.
Diaper-pattern brickwork.
Stair dormers on one-and-a-half-story houses.
Virginia:
Gambrel hipped above wind beam.
Jerkin-head roof.
Narrow vertical windows.
Outside chimneys clearing gables.
North Carolina: (Albemarle):
Characteristic shed dormer and rear extension.
Turned posts in place of classical columns.
Diaper-pattern brickwork (north-central).
Moravian: Flemish bond, small windows, segmental-arch heads; bracketed doorway hoods.

South Carolina: (Charleston):
Tinted stucco, red pantiles.
West Indian piazza, one-story, wood.
Chimneys in longitudinal walls.
Jerkin-head roof.
End-entrance, two-story piazza.

External Earmarks of Early Georgian

Balanced façade.
Imposing doorway with pilasters and cornice or pediment (broken pediment indicates baroque influence).
Door paneled, with lights in top or in transom above.
Door side lights *outside* pilasters.
Large sash windows with small panes (18 to 24), slender muntins.
Windows framed by architrave, sometimes with flat cornice or triangular pediment.
Windows without blinds, North or South.
Windows with solid shutters (Middle Colonies only).
Round-topped window over stair landing.
Low-pitched roof. Ridge roof may have flat deck with balustrade. Many have cupola.
Cornice with modillions, moldings, and perhaps dentils.
Dormers narrow, pedimented (in South hip-roofed).
Alternate triangular and segmental pediments.
High foundation.

External Earmarks of Late Georgian

Balanced façade.
Doorways flanked by pilasters or engaged columns.
Doorways with side lights *inside* pilasters.
Fanlight over both door and side lights.
Door entablature may have triglyphs, mutules, guttae.

187. The Dutch stoep or stoop consisted of a small pillared porch furnished with a pair of flanking benches.

Doorway may have pediment on brackets—or portico (two-story portico in South).

Door may be surmounted by semicircular lunette.

Doorway may be surmounted by Palladian window.

May have louvered blinds.

House may have projecting central pavilion with pedimented gable.

House may have pilasters full height of façade.

Roof balustrade may be Chinese lattice (very late).

Roof may have cupola.

Semicircular headed dormers occasional.

High foundation, possibly with water table marked by molded bricks.

May have string course (second-floor line) marked by projecting brick, or stone belt course.

Stone: regular coursed ashlar—or rough stone stuccoed over.

Brick: quoins at corners.

Woodwork may be rusticated.

External Earmarks of Federal Style (1790-1820)

Quiet, dignified design with delicate decorative detail.

Geometric motifs.

Painted brick or stucco.

Brick stuccoed to resemble stone.

Large portico, narrow side lights, wide ellipti-

188. Early Dutch doors often had "bull's-eye" lights in the upper panels.

cal fanlight.

Curved or polygonal bays on exterior walls.

Balustrade or parapet located above eaves.

High foundation; water table and string course marked.

Low-pitched roof.

Earmarks of Greek Revival

Portico with single or two-story Greek classical columns or heavy square pillars, or

Fully pedimented gable.

Doors with side lights covered by transom, all framed by flat pilasters and architrave.

Corniced eaves.

Tall main façade windows.

Pilastered corners.

May have eyebrow windows in architrave—or decorative gratings.

Recessed porch with pillars (regional).

Corner pilasters with roof cornice returned to complete order.

Main entrance in gable end (occasional).

Two-story porch with pediment and railed veranda common in South.

High, hipped roof with two or four chimneys common in South (1790-1820).

NOTE: Variations are extreme. A plain, small house with a porch, having two square pillars, a plain architrave, and a simple cornice may be regarded as a modified example of the Greek Revival style. So, too, may a severely plain masonry house with nothing more than a simple cornice, plain lintels and window sills, and a recessed, pilastered door-

189. Colonial doorways with flat architrave, 3-pane transom, and sunken panels date from about 1850.

190. In mid-18th-century Pennsylvania a double-leaf, lined door might have the outer boards set in a chevron pattern, often accompanied by hardware in a style peculiar to the locality, as in this example.

way with full-width rectangular transom and sidelights.

Some Regional Characteristics

Northern

Gambrels used on New England mansions, mostly English origin.

Gambrels rare in Pennsylvania. Where used are of Swedish type.

Gable roof with "Dutch kick", a Flemish innovation in New York and New Jersey.

Bell-cast gambrel with pents of German origin (Pennsylvania).

Pent roofs, introduced by Pennsylvania Germans.

Beam-and-plank construction (heavy beams instead of joists; plank floors, of Dutch origin, New York and New Jersey.

Bracketed posts supporting floor beams, a Dutch feature, New York.

Bed-places built in, Dutch, Hudson Valley, New York.

Stone gables clapboarded above windbeam, Dutch, New York and New Jersey.

Door hoods without brackets (cantilevered), Dutch in New York, German in Pennsylvania.

Double-row transom lights, Dutch.

"Tombstone" transom and door lights, Dutch.

Heavily molded fireplace lintels, early Dutch.

Tiled fireplace surrounds and cheeks, Dutch.

Joists resting on top of girders a Pennsylvania German feature.

Half-timber framing (brick-filled) used by Pennsylvania Germans (including Moravians).

Cantilevered door hoods paneled on underside, Pennsylvania, German.

Door panels carved inside, Pennsylvania German.

Summer beams in New England run from gable end to chimney, except in Massachusetts where they run from front to back of house.

In Pennsylvania, Greek Revival houses of central-hall type predominate.

In New England, Greek Revival houses of side-hall, gable type predominate.

Swan's-neck pediment over front doors, originated in the Connecticut Valley.

Georgian houses in New England, mostly wood; some brick.

Georgian houses in Pennsylvania, New York, and New Jersey mostly stone; some brick.

Georgian houses elsewhere mostly brick, usually laid in Flemish bond.

191. Mid-18th-century New England doorways often relied more on form and proportion than on decoration. This example from Wethersfield, Connecticut is dated about 1750.

Southern

Hipped gambrel used in Virginia exclusively. Gambrels used in Virginia after 1700, Maryland type.

Jerkin-head roof (clipped gable) used in North Carolina, South Carolina, Virginia, and Maryland.

Gable-on-hip roof is characteristic of French plantation style.

Chimney pents found only on Maryland exterior chimneys.

Spacing of end chimneys from gables a Virginia feature.

All-header brick bond used in Annapolis, Maryland.

"Single-house" plan unique to Charleston, South Carolina.

Greek Revival houses (medium size), two-story height preferred in South.

French Colonial houses of "raised cottage" type, with basements above ground, found only in New Orleans.

French Louisiana plantation houses evolved from raised cottages.

Turned posts often used in North Carolina in place of classical columns for verandas.

Diaper-patterned brickwork in North Carolina copied from Maryland and New Jersey.

Painted stucco indigenous to South Carolina.

Red pantiles indigenous to South Carolina.

Gambrels not used on important buildings in South, or on houses over one story high.

End-wall chimneys unusual in South Carolina.

Stair dormers an exclusively Southern invention.

192. This simple, pedimented doorway with sunken panels and semicircular fanlight is in South Britain, Connecticut, but the same style was popular in Virginia and North Carolina.

193. A country carpenter's version of a small late-Georgian doorway, the dummy fanlight carved in wood. Nantucket, about 1790.

Tropical piazza originated in Charleston.

Two-story porticoes originated in South (early).

Cast-iron balconies and decorative ironwork manufactured in Pennsylvania, 1840.

Half-timber framing (brick-filled) used by English in early Jamestown, Virginia.

Greek Revival houses of central-hall type predominate in the South.

Midwest and Western

Greek Revival houses of side entrance type predominate in Ohio.

Greek Revival houses (medium size), of one story or a story and a half preferred in Midwest.

Redwood shakes used on early California houses.

Cantilevered verandas used on two-story California houses.

Flat red tiles used on California houses.

Adobe houses in California often tinted with colored "whitewash."

New England "saltboxes" found in California in 1850 s.

194. In Rhode Island, noted for its beautiful doorways, this is one of the best in Late Georgian (1804) style. The Captain Richard Barney house, Wickford.

195. LaTourette, New Jersey—a 1730 house having Dutch-Swedish characteristics was brought up to date with the modified Federal doorway (1800 to 1825) whose style borders on that of the Greek Revival.

196. A Federal doorway of 1837, with full-width carved dummy fanlight, and shutters on the side lights—an unusual design.

197. Many late-Victorian doors throughout the country had heavy bracketed hoods such as the one shown here—and the decorated glass panels as well.

198. The doorway of the Porter house, Hadley, Massachusetts, which no doubt originally had a fancy Connecticut-River-style latch— the kind of doorway that gave traditional houses a Georgian air.

GLOSSARY

ANCHOR IRON: an iron bar or ring, usually decorative in design, used with a bolt to hold a masonry wall tight to a wood beam. Also called a beam iron.

ANTAE (singular, ANTA): pilasters in which base and capital do not conform with the columns of the building, usually placed at the end of a side wall.

ANTHEMION: a flat ornamental design arranged in radiating clusters, usually based on the flowers of the honeysuckle; found in Greek architecture.

ARCHITRAVE: the lowermost section of a classical entablature, resting on the columns. Also applied to band or molding carried around window or door opening.

ASHLAR: hewn or squared stone, usually in large blocks, used in courses. Called random ashlar when sizes of blocks vary.

BALLOON FRAME: house frame built up from small-dimensioned lumber, principally two-by-fours, nailed together.

BALUSTER: a turned or rectangular upright supporting a stair handrail or forming part of a balustrade.

BALUSTRADE: a row of balusters topped by a rail.

BARGEBOARD: a board covering the end rafters of a gable. Also called a verge board.

BAROQUE: an elaborate and ornate architectural style found in various countries during the late Renaissance.

BATTEN DOOR: a door composed of two or more vertical boards held together by horizontal wooden strips.

BEAD: a convex, rounded molding, usually semicircular in section.

BED-PLACE: a recess in the wall of a Dutch Colonial house into which a bed is built.

BEEHIVE OVEN: an external bake oven, shaped like a circular beehive.

BOLECTION MOLDING: a molding which projects beyond the general surface of a panel or connects two varying surface levels.

BONDING: in brickwork or stonework, the binding of the pieces together by overlapping lengthwise and in thickness.

BORNING ROOM: a main-floor room off the keeping room, reserved for births because its proximity to kitchen fireplace provided warmth and an accessible source of hot water.

BRACED FRAME: a house frame of massive timbers, jointed and pegged together, and braced by lighter members in the angles.

BRACKET: a curved or angular projection at the top of a post for support of a horizontal section. Also, a scroll at the end of a step in an open-string stair.

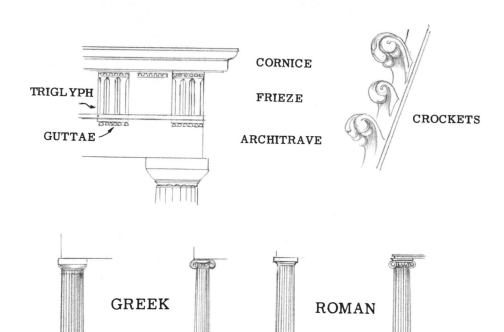

CORNICE

FRIEZE

ARCHITRAVE

TRIGLYPH

GUTTAE

CROCKETS

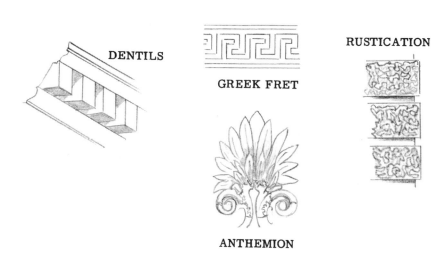

GREEK

DORIC   IONIC

ROMAN

DORIC   IONIC

DENTILS

GREEK FRET

ANTHEMION

RUSTICATION

BRICK BONDS

ENGLISH

FLEMISH

COMMON

DUTCH CROSS

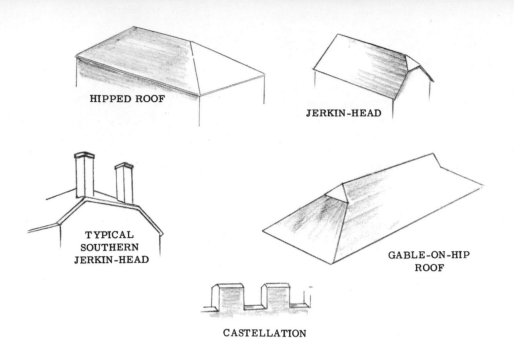

HIPPED ROOF

JERKIN-HEAD

TYPICAL
SOUTHERN
JERKIN-HEAD

GABLE-ON-HIP
ROOF

CASTELLATION

GAMBRELS

NOTE: Proportions vary according to depth of house.

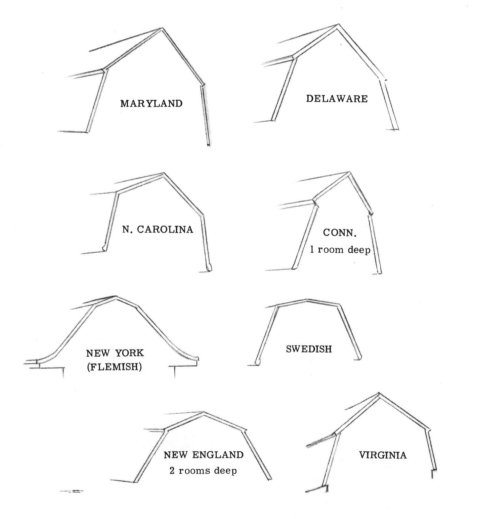

MARYLAND

DELAWARE

N. CAROLINA

CONN.
1 room deep

NEW YORK
(FLEMISH)

SWEDISH

NEW ENGLAND
2 rooms deep

VIRGINIA

BRICK NOGGING: bricks used to fill in between wall studs as insulation.

CANTILEVERED DOOR HOOD: a hood supported at the wall end only, needing neither posts nor brackets.

CAP: the protective or finishing member at the top of a post, wall, or window.

CAPE COD STYLE: that of the single-story early New England house originating in Massachusetts, with center chimney, the pitched roof coming down to first floor ceiling level.

CARPENTERS' GOTHIC: a Gothic-revival house built of wood, with sawn or turned decorative members.

CASED-IN TIMBER: a beam or post which has been boxed or covered, to improve its appearance.

CASEMENT WINDOW: a window sash opening outward on side hinges.

CASTELLATED: having a battlemented parapet or roof.

CATSLIDE: the long rear roof of a lean-to house (Southern). Also applied to the house itself.

CHAIR RAIL: a wooden molding on a wall at chair height, designed to protect wall from damage by chair backs.

CHIMNEY: clustered: separate flues gathered together at chimney top; pilastered: a rectangular chimney with one or more separate flues attached to it above the roof.

CLAPBOARD: board siding laid horizontally, and overlapping; butted vertically. The lower edge is usually thicker than the upper one.

CLAY-AND-HAIR MORTAR: clay mixed with animal hair; the earliest kind of mortar used for masonry.

CORBEL: a supporting projection on the face of a wall.

CORBEL STEPS: bricks arranged in steps to form the top of a gable wall. (Sometimes called corbie or crow steps.)

CORNER BOARD: a board nailed vertically over the corner post of a braced frame house, against which the siding terminates.

CORNICE: (a) a molding at the edge of a roof; (b) a molding that covers the angle formed by ceiling and wall; (c) the uppermost section of an entablature.

COURSE: a horizontal row of bricks, stones, shingles, etc.

COURSED STONE: laid in horizontal layers.

COVE MOLDING: a concave molding.

CROCKET: a Gothic ornament in stone, carved like a fern frond—often used on pinnacles. Copied in wood in Victorian architecture.

CROSS-GABLE: a gable set parallel to the roof ridge.

CROSSETTES: decorative square offsets at the upper corners of a door or window architrave. Also called "ears."

CUPOLA: a lookout or similar small structure on the top of a building.

DADO: (a) lower part of the wall below the chair rail; (b) space on an architectural pedestal between base and surbase.

DENTIL: a small, rectangular block forming one of a series applied as an ornament below a cornice.

DRESSED STONE: see ashlar.

DRIP COURSE: a projecting course of masonry serving to deflect rainwater from a wall or structural opening or joint beneath it. Also called dripstone.

DORMER WINDOW: a window that projects from a roof. Among the various kinds are: shed, doghouse (ridge-roofed), pedimented stair.

DOUBLE DOOR: a door divided vertically into two leaves, one of them being hung on each side of a doorway, the two sections meeting in the middle.

DUTCH BRICK: a small-sized brick, most commonly $1\frac{1}{2}$x3x7", although there are other sizes.

EYEBROW WINDOWS

CHIMNEY PENT

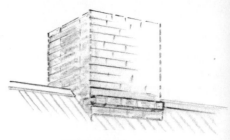

CHIMNEY DRIP-COURSE

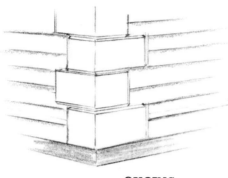

QUOINS

BEADED CLAPBOARDS

PENDILL

PILASTERED CHIMNEY

ANCHOR IRON

PILASTER

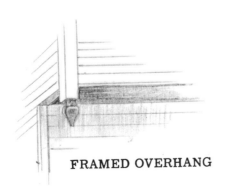

FRAMED OVERHANG

DATE PANEL

CANTILEVERED HOOD

DUTCH CROSS BOND: a method of laying bricks so that they present a definite pattern. See illustration.

DUTCH KICK: the tilt of the eaves in a pitched-roof house, typical of Dutch and Flemish architecture.

DUTCH OVEN: a cooking utensil. Frequently erroneously applied to the bake oven of a fireplace.

DUTCH STOEP: a small wooden porch, usually with two benches, covered by a cantilevered door hood. Colloquially: stoop.

ECHINUS: the curved projecting molding supporting the uppermost section in a Greek Doric capital.

ENGAGED COLUMNS: columns almost but not quite detached from the wall behind them.

ENGLISH BOND: Bricks laid in alternate courses of headers and stretchers. See illustration.

ENTABLATURE: the architrave, frieze, and cornice resting on the capitals of columns.

ENTASIS: a slight convex curvature given to the taper of a column to make the sides appear as straight lines.

EYEBROW WINDOW: the low, inward-opening, bottom-hinged sash inserted in the architrave of a Greek Revival house at upper floor level. Also called "lie-on-your-stomach" window.

FAÇADE: the face or front of a building.

FANLIGHT: a fan-shaped window above the door frame in Georgian houses.

FEATHER-EDGED: a board tapered to a fine edge to fit into a groove in another board.

FEDERAL STYLE: a refined, severely classical form of the late Georgian (1810–1830) architectural style.

FENESTRATION: the arrangement and proportioning of windows in a house wall.

FIREPLACE CHEEKS: the splayed sides of a fireplace.

FIXED SASH: a window sash that is made to remain closed.

FLEMISH BOND: bricks laid with headers and stretchers alternating in the same course.

FLEMISH SWEEP: a turned-up eave; often called the "Dutch kick" but erroneously identified with Dutch architecture.

FRAMED OVERHANG: an upper section of a house overhanging the one below it as a result of having horizontal timbers extend beyond the vertical face of the section below.

FRET: an ornamental pattern cut into or through a flat surface.

FRETWORK: ornamental openwork in wood, stone, or iron.

FRIEZE: (a) the upper part of a wall, below the cornice and above the paneling; (b) that part of an entablature found between the architrave and the cornice.

GABLE: the end wall of a house having a pitched or gambrel roof.

GAMBREL ROOF: a form of ridge roof with two pitches.

GARRISON HOUSE: one with a framed front overhang at the second-floor level.

GEORGIAN STYLE: the formal classical architecture of the 18th and early 19th centuries.

GINGERBREAD: decorative woodwork applied to Victorian houses.

GIRT: a beam framed into the posts of a braced-frame house at upper-floor level; it may be a front, rear, chimney, or end girt.

GOTHIC: pertaining to an architectural style of the Middle Ages characterized by the pointed arch.

GOTHIC REVIVAL: an adaptation of the Gothic style to domestic architecture in early 19th-century America.

GREEK REVIVAL: an architectural style based on Greek classicism which, in America, came into flower in the early 19th century.

GUTTA: on a Doric entablature, one of a series of decorations, rounded as a rule, found on the underside of a mutule.

HALF-HOUSE: half of a central-chimney house (including the chimney), built with the idea of later adding a like section the other side of the chimney.

HALF-TIMBERED FRAME HOUSE: a house built of heavy timbers, the exterior ones left exposed, with spaces between beams filled with withes and clay, or with brick, to form exterior walls.

HELLENIC: the last period of classical Greek architecture.

HEWN OVERHANG: a floor overhanging the wall below it as a result of the lower vertical timbers being cut back.

HIPPED ROOF: a roof that slopes back equally from each end of the building so that there are no gables.

HOOD: a projection or roof over a doorway.

HUDSON RIVER BRACKETED: (colloquial) an expression applied to heavily ornamented Victorian houses in the Hudson River Valley of New York.

JACOBEAN STYLE: a period of early English Renaissance architecture lasting approximately throughout the reign of James I.

JAMB: the masonry, brick, or wood lining or vertical surround of a window, fireplace, or doorway.

JERKIN-HEAD ROOF: a clipped or truncated gable, i.e., a roof which is hipped for only part of its height.

JETTY: an overhang.

JOIST: any small timber laid horizontally to support a floor or ceiling.

KEEPING ROOM: the old-time name for the common or living room.

KEYSTONE: the central, tapered masonry member of an arch, which acts as a wedge to keep the arch from collapsing.

LEAN-TO HOUSE: a house with a rear shed addition whose roof is a continuation of the house roof, thus forming one long slope. Also called a catslide or saltbox house.

LIE-ON-YOUR-STOMACH WINDOWS: a colloquial name for eyebrow windows.

LIGHTS: window panes.

LINTEL: a horizontal member spanning an opening.

LOUVERS: elongated vents or horizontal slats in an opening which admit air but not light.

LUNETTE: a semicircular space in a window or under an arch.

LYRE-MOTIF: a design in the form of a lyre.

MANSARD ROOF: sometimes called a French roof. Has two slopes, the lower one being steeper than the upper. Unlike the gambrel, it always has four sides, so that there is no gable.

METOPE: the space between two triglyphs in a Doric frieze, left open in early work but later decorated by carving.

MODILLION: an ornamental block or bracket applied to the underside of a projecting cornice.

MULLION: a heavy dividing bar of wood or stone between sections of a window.

MUNTIN: a small, slender wood or metal member to hold the glass in a window sash.

MUTULE: a projecting block above the triglyph on the underside of a Doric cornice.

OCTAGONAL HOUSE: one having eight sides; specifically a Victorian design promoted by Orson Fowler.

ORIEL WINDOW: a small bay window usually supported by corbels or brackets.

OVERHANG: see hewn overhang; framed overhang; jetty.

PALLADIAN ARCHITECTURE: a generic term for classical architecture during the 18th century and widely adopted in England following publication of the designs of the Italian architect, Andrea Palladio.

PALLADIAN WINDOW: a group of three sashes, the center one being higher and having a rounded top, named after its inventor, Andrea Palladio, the 16th-century architect. Formerly called the Venetian window.

PARAPET: a low wall at the edge of a roof

or gable.

PARQUET FLOOR: a flooring composed of wood blocks.

PAVILION: a projecting section of a façade designed to give architectural emphasis.

PEDIMENT: the triangular space forming the gable of a two-pitched roof; a similar form used over porticoes, doors, windows, etc. including curved, scroll, broken, and swan's neck varieties.

PENDILLS: carved drops formed at the lower ends of second-floor posts in a framed overhang.

PENT ROOF: a narrow, continuous shed roof attached to a wall; usually, although not always, found at second-floor level. Sometimes it is carried across the gable ends of the house to the eaves.

PILASTER: an upright, flat, rectangular pillar projecting only slightly from a wall, and designed to simulate a column with a capital, shaft, and base.

PLANK HOUSE: one built without studs, in place of which, wide board planks are used vertically. Plastered within; and covered with clapboards or shingles without.

PLATE: the horizontal wooden member that lies along the top of a wall, or forms the topmost member of a braced frame that supports the rafters.

POLYGONAL: having many angles.

PORTICO: a covered or roofed space at the entrance of a building. In a classical portico the roof pediment is supported by columns.

QUATREFOIL: an ornamental design, having four lobes or arcs supported by cusps.

QUOINS: heavy blocks, generally of stone, or of wood cut to imitate stone. used at the corner of a building to reinforce masonry walls, or in wood as a decorative feature.

RAINBOW ROOF: a roof in which the rafters are arched to give more headroom and better resistance to wind pressure; found on Cape Cod and Nantucket Island, Massachusetts.

RETURN: a term applied to a right-angle turn in a molding or other applied feature of a building, such as a cornice.

RIDGE BOARD: a board placed vertically between the top ends of rafters to form a roof ridge.

ROMAN CLASSICISM: the use of Roman classical detail in architecture.

ROSETTE: a rose-shaped patera.

RUSTICATED: a term applied to masonry in which the edges of a joint are chamfered or recessed, giving the appearance of a wide joint; also to the tooling of a stone surface.

SALTBOX HOUSE: a one-and-a-half or two-story house with long rear roof line. Also known as a lean-to or catslide house. So called because it was said to resemble an old Colonial salt box.

SCROLLWORK: thin wood cut into designs with a scrollsaw and applied as decoration.

SEGMENTED PEDIMENT: a pediment in the form of a segmental arch, i.e., one not a complete semicircle.

SHAKES: an early term for split wood shingles.

SHEATHING: a layer of boards on the outside of a house frame, over which the finish siding and roofing are applied.

SIDE LIGHTS: a vertical line of small glass panes flanking a doorway.

SIDING: exterior wall covering.

SILL: (a) the bottom-most horizontal timber of a wall; (b) the exterior horizontal member on which a window frame rests.

STAIR DORMER: a wide dormer built to accommodate the upper part of a staircase giving access to a "half floor" or roof space.

STEAMBOAT GOTHIC: a term applied to Victorian Gothic houses with vertical battened siding.

STRINGCOURSE: a continuous horizontal band, either plain or molded, projecting from the surface of a building at an upper floor level. Sometimes called a belt course.

STRINGER: a side member of a staircase against which the steps abut.

SUMMER BEAM: the massive principal floor beam usually extending from an end girt to a chimney girt to enable short joists to be used. In Massachusetts the beam runs from a front girt to a rear girt.

TENON: the end of a wooden member cut to form a projection that fits into a corresponding hole or mortise in another piece.

THREE-QUARTER HOUSE: a house with a "central" chimney off center.

TIE BEAM: a beam extending between a pair of roof rafters to prevent them from bending inward or spreading at the feet. Also called a wind beam.

TOMBSTONE LIGHT: a small window in a transom over a doorway, with lights in the shape of an arched tombstone.

TRANSOM: in Colonial architecture, a window with small lights over an exterior door.

TREFOIL: a form of tracery having three arcs separated from each other by cusps; a decorative window divided into three lobes.

TRIGLYPH: a decorative block with three vertical grooves in a Doric frieze.

TRIPLE WINDOW: three windows massed together, all of the same height. NOT the same as a Palladian window.

TUDOR: pertaining to the period in English history from 1485 to 1603.

TYMPANUM: the triangular space surrounded by the cornice or molding of a pediment.

VERGE BOARD: see Bargeboard.

WATER TABLE: a brick or stone setback on an exterior wall, usually at the foundation level.

WAINSCOT: wood paneling applied to interior wall.

WEATHERBOARDING: clapboarding.

WESTERN RESERVE: a tract of 3,500,000 acres of land near Lake Erie reserved to Connecticut on cession of Northwest Territory to United States. Now part of Ohio.

WIND BEAM: see tie beam.

CREDITS

For their kind permission to use the photographs listed here, the authors are grateful to:

The New-York Historical Society
   Figs. 24, 43, 83, 187, 188, 190

Philadelphia Museum of Art
   Fig. 61

Mr. Chas. E. Peterson, National Park Service
   Figs. 103, 123, 168, 190

Mr. C. Clayton Andrews, Architect
   Figs. 147, 148

New York State Education Department
   Figs. 37, 39

Historic American Buildings Survey, Library of Congress
   Frontispiece and Figs. 4, 5, 8, 14, 20, 26, 27, 30, 31, 32, 36, 40, 42, 44, 46, 48, 52 (Mr. S. P. Mixon), 53, 54, 57, 58, 63, 64, 66, 73, 74, 75, 76, 78, 80, 82, 84, 85, 86, 87, 88, 90, 91, 92, 94, 95, 96, 98, 99, 101, 102, 104 (Mr. A. W. LeBoeuf), 105, 109 (Mr. E. H. Pickering), 110, 111 (Mr. C. O. Greene), 112, 113, 114, 121, 122, 124, 126, 127, 128, 131, 132, 133, 135, 136, 137, 138, 139, 140, 141, 143, 144, 145 146, 149, 150, 163, 173, 174, 175, 176, 177, 178, 179, 180, 181, 183, 194, 195, 198

INDEX